THE
ANARCHIST
COOKBOOK

THE ANARCHIST COOKBOOK

A TOOLKIT TO PROTEST AND PEACEFUL RESISTANCE

AAKAR PATEL

Illustrations by PenPencilDraw

HarperCollins *Publishers* India

First published in India by HarperCollins *Publishers* 2022
4th Floor, Tower A, Building No. 10, Phase II, DLF Cyber City,
Gurugram, Haryana – 122002
www.harpercollins.co.in

2 4 6 8 10 9 7 5 3 1

Copyright © Aakar Patel and PenPencilDraw 2022

P-ISBN: 978-93-5489-325-4
E-ISBN: 978-93-5489-330-8

The views and opinions expressed in this book are the authors' own.
The facts are as reported by them and the publishers
are not in any way liable for the same.

Aakar Patel and PenPencilDraw assert the moral rights
to be identified as the authors of this work.

All rights reserved. No part of this publication may be reproduced,
stored in a retrieval system, or transmitted, in any form or by any
means, electronic, mechanical, photocopying, recording or otherwise,
without the prior permission of the publishers.

Typeset in 11.5/15.7 Dante MT Std at
Manipal Technologies Limited, Manipal

Printed and bound at
Thomson Press (India) Ltd.

*Dedicated to the Bhima Koregaon 16
and to the memory of Father Stan Swamy*

Contents

SECTION I: SHRINKING SPACES

1. Are You a (Dis)engaged Citizen?   3
2. The Past Is Still Present   10
3. At the Edge of Autocracy   26
4. The Crumbling Pillars of Democracy   40
5. Beginning Your Activism Journey   45

SECTION II: HOW TO COOK

6. Are You Ready to Stir Things Up?   53
7. The Not-So-Secret Sauce of Activism   57
8. The Key Ingredients   69
9. The Hidden Hazards   81
10. Make It to MasterChef Level   89
11. Put Your Hand Up   97

SECTION III: SUCCESSFUL PROTESTS OF OUR TIME (AND WHAT YOU CAN LEARN FROM THEM)

12. It Was One Tweet — 109
13. The Strength of Unbroken Resistance — 114
14. 'I Can't Breathe' — 122
15. Your Mother, You Take Care of Her — 128
16. This Land Is My Land — 134
17. Never Too Small to Make a Difference — 141
18. Morcha for Change — 146
19. A Lost Battle — 158

SECTION IV: LAWLESS LAWS

20. Dangerous until Proven Innocent — 167
21. Rewriting the Law — 173

SECTION V: UNDERSTAND YOUR PRIVILEGE AND USE IT FOR CHANGE

22. Why India Needs Us to Protest — 207

Notes — 231
About the Author and Illustrator — 255

SECTION I

Shrinking Spaces

1

Are You a (Dis)engaged Citizen?

Let us begin with a question: What is our relationship with the State? A word that we can take to mean the government, whether local or central. For some of us, such as those writing and likely reading this, the points at which the State intersects with our lives are few. This is the upper class (only 3 per cent of India pays income tax[1] so we cannot speak properly of a middle class—only an upper and the rest). Professionally, this class operates in English, the language of this book, and lives in the cities of India. English, which nine of ten Indians do not speak, allows those of us who do speak it and work in it to be global. In cultural and even professional ways, we are inhabitants of a wider world than the majority of Indians.

Physically, our lives are less touched by the State than is the case for most Indians. We are unlikely to have been educated in government schools and our children have not spent time in anganwadis. Our health is taken care of by the private sector and its doctors and hospitals, not by the nearly ten lakh women who are Accredited Social Health Activists (ASHAs). Our reliance on the Public Distribution System (PDS), through which the State gives out subsidized grain, is likely to be low or non-existent. Eighty crore people, two-thirds of India, benefit from PDS[2], which gives individuals either five kilograms of rice (for ₹3 per kilogram) or five kilograms of wheat (at ₹2 per kilogram) every month. Over twenty crore Indians are still undernourished[3] because their access to State help is inadequate or absent. This book's readers are unlikely to be among them.

The flat we live in does not have a toilet built with government subsidy. We do not use public transport systems—particularly the cheaper mediums such as intra- and inter-city buses—as much as most of the population does. Many of us have abandoned trains for planes. So the deterioration in rail services—a third of all India's trains ran late in 2018[4]—does not affect us much. When the Union government eased Covid-19 restrictions, it allowed airlines to fly at full capacity but ran fewer than three hundred of its sixteen thousand daily trains for several months.[5] Even in a global crisis, 'we'—and it is appropriate to see ourselves as a privileged club of life members—were either unaffected or less affected than the many by the actions of the State.

And then there are the negative points of contact with the State. Here, again, our club is not touched by the criminal justice system as many Indians are. Both in the number of times that we are in contact with it and in the way we are. We may not be familiar with some of the peculiar features of India's criminal justice system, such as administrative detention. Also known as preventive detention, this is how the Indian State holds, for months and often years, individuals without a crime or a trial. They are locked up on the mere suspicion of the State and its agents—the police and the bureaucracy—that if free, these individuals may commit an offence in the future. There are, in fact, multiple laws in each Indian state, as we shall see in the next chapter, that allows it and the Centre to keep citizens locked up in such a manner. We, or those we know, have rarely been subjected

ARE YOU A (DIS)ENGAGED CITIZEN?

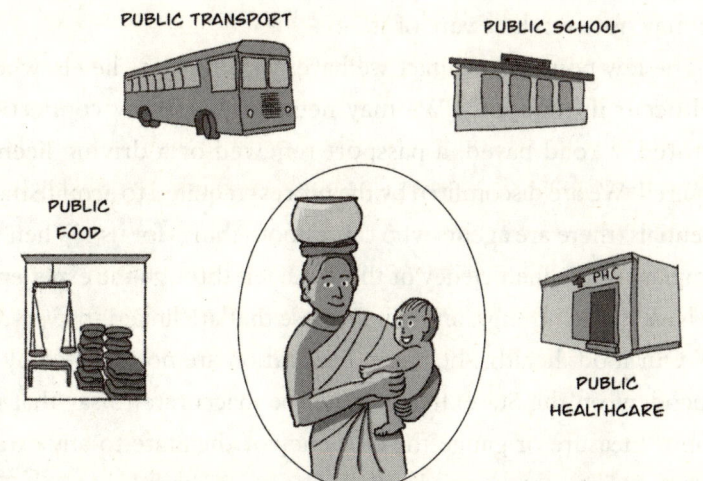

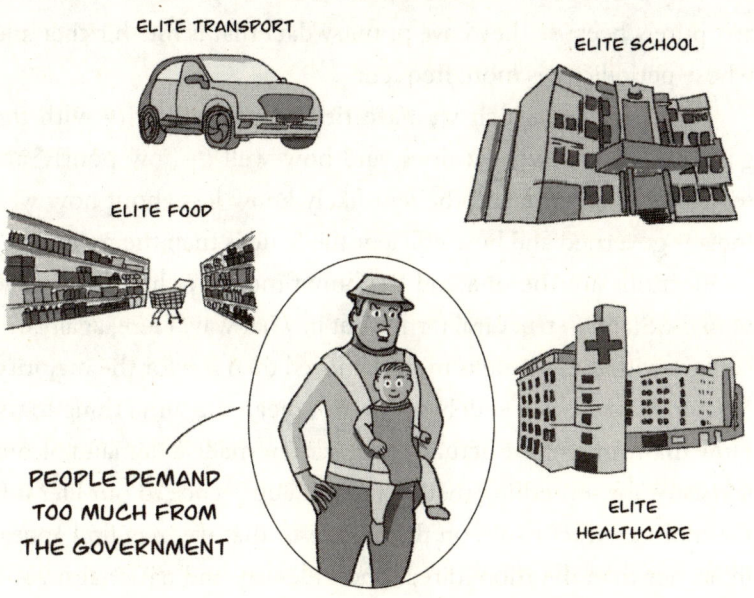

to a system of justice where there is punishment without a crime. We may not even be aware of it.

The few points of contact we have with the State lie elsewhere and occur infrequently. We may need an electricity connection restored, a road paved, a passport renewed or a driving licence acquired. We are discomfited by the process required to acquire these essentials (there are agents who can smooth things for us). When we complain of the inefficiency of the State, it is through the experience we have in such things, and not in those that are linked to everyday life. Our food, health, shelter and education are not affected by or dependent on the State. It would not be inaccurate to say that we cannot measure or gauge the efficiency of the State to any extent because we are not engaged with it in any meaningful measure. The majority is more informed about the reality of governance than we are, purely because they have primary data that is much richer and whose periodicity is more frequent.

The spaces in which we have first-hand familiarity with the government and what it does, and how well or how poorly, are scarce. We, the elite and the few, likely know less about how well India is governed and how efficient the State is than the many.

Elections are the one and the only time we politically engage with the State in structural terms. But in what way? Here, again, our contact with the system is more removed than it is for the majority. Electoral promises and delivery do not mean the same thing to us. How many of us have actually met with or made a demand of our legislator for something that will make a difference to our life? It is the more abstract issues on the manifesto that we may find appeal in, rather than the more direct ones. Identity and nationalism and India's status in the world are important and substantial things for an elite that considers itself, and in many ways is, global. A seat on the UN Security Council, or the threat of firm military action from a strong and firm and decisive figure.

The charisma of leadership and the power of speech is to us an actual and real reason to vote for someone. Their performance in office is incidental, perhaps even irrelevant.

To put it crudely, we engage with politics the way we do with Bollywood. The appeal of the politician is similar to, and perhaps the same as, the appeal of the film star. The depth of engagement from the audience is also the same. No delivery in the real world is expected of either; the performance on screen is all there is. It is entertainment and the performer appeals to our emotions—our likes, hates, loves and prejudices—more than they affect our actual, lived reality.

If we had to deal with a government whose insistence on linking Aadhaar to the receipt of PDS grain affected us, we might not view politics and political figures in a different manner. A full 10 per cent or more of those entitled to receiving PDS grain cannot access it because the eroded fingerprints on their hardworking hands are not recognized by the system.[6]

We do not know what it must be like to not have agency over what language our children are schooled in. Many Indians do not have a choice over their medium of education. And there's no guarantee that if they pick what they want, they will actually get it. Many schools in North India, according to the Sachar Committee Report of 2006, have Urdu teachers with no knowledge of Urdu.[7]

Our world of transport which has 100 million annual plane journeys is more efficient by far than the world of the railways with its eight billion train journeys. The facilities, efficiencies, conveniences and public transport linkages that are provided for us, the elite, exceed both in absolute terms and certainly in terms of per capita usage than what is given to the rest. Our resources are skewed towards what we, the few, need and insist on.

Mumbai has two airports and Delhi three. But Chhattisgarh and Madhya Pradesh don't even have a statewide bus network.[8] They were shut down ostensibly because the states could not get them to turn a profit. How are the poor in those states, whose combined population is more than Germany's, expected to travel? They can figure it out themselves. There is no such expectation of profit from projects such as bullet trains. The Airports Authority of India loses money on the majority of the airports it manages.[9] It can carry on, presumably because it is more essential than state bus services.

And so, it seems safe to conclude that our engagement with the State and participation in its functioning is low. The State can carry on operating in those aspects we are uninterested in and do what it sees fit without resistance from us, the most influential Indians. There are several areas in which governance may have deteriorated but has not been noticed by those of us unconcerned with the areas. We do not know what it is doing in those areas, or at least we do not know it first-hand.

The fact is that for reasons relating to the economy of the media and the sort of audience advertisers seek, a small elite controls the narrative in India. In those spaces where this elite has no interest, or has an interest that is in opposition to that of the masses, the state of governance is poor and in decline.

But this may not even be acknowledged and therefore would not have a chance of being corrected. Things would continue as they were. The State would remain disconnected and the democratic pressure which should build on it for self-correction would not be as strong because of an absence of interest and ignorance from the elite. If Delhi's airports were to be shut tomorrow because they couldn't turn a profit, there would be an uproar. And rightly so. But for many of the other issues of equal and perhaps even exceeding importance, there is no resistance to what the State does. We must understand why this is the case. Its roots lie in the history and origins of the modern Indian State.

2

The Past Is Still Present

What Jawaharlal Nehru and the Congress inherited on 14 August 1947 was an aggressively expansionist imperialist State. It had taken, usually through annexation, deception and war, large parts of the subcontinent never previously under Delhi's rule.

The rights of this occupying colonial State were naturally more important than the rights of the occupied. This was reflected in the State's legislations, statues and procedures. The duty of the State was not to ensure the rule of law, as democracies promise themselves, but *law and order*. This is the term by which Indians are more familiar with the apparatus that carries words and phrases like lathicharge, band-o-bust (a Farsi word meaning 'arrangement', literally, to tie and bind) and curfew. These are terms and actions from the State that the citizens of most liberal democracies are unfamiliar with. The physical suppression of the population is not natural to the civilized world.

Democratic India struggled to figure out the manner in which it was different from the colonial state. Legislatures existed before 1947, laws were written by Indians, elections were held, people voted,

LAW & ORDER

FEELS A LITTLE SMALL

Indians had access to justice and to free expression. The franchise was limited and not all adults could vote. The scope of legislation was limited and so were the powers of the elected. But they were actually elected, and amid few or no accusations of rigging or cheating. The Government of India Act of 1935 is quite similar to the Indian Constitution in many ways. It lays out the ways in which the State is to function. And in most ways, the State functioned then in the same manner as it does today. The rights of the State continue to be more important than the rights of its citizens.

This is why the laws and regulations under which Indians are governed today are essentially the same as those we had as a subject people. This lack of imagination about what to do as a free nation is true not just of India but the wider subcontinent. That is why the laws in India are almost the same, more or less, as they are in Pakistan. This is true particularly of the criminal justice system. The Lahori or Karachiwallah is as familiar with the numbers 420, 302 and 144 as are the people in Kolkata or Chennai. These are numbers given to laws written by Thomas Macaulay more than a century-and-a-half ago, enacted just after the mutiny in which the Raj crushed the Indian freedom spirit. So if the laws were the same, and not just in India but the subcontinent, what is the difference between the Republic of India and the Raj? Surely, as a free people, we should have given ourselves more liberty than our foreign rulers did?

IT'S TWINS!

Actually, we did. This is the one area in which the Indian Constitution diverges the most from the Act of 1935 and the other documents through which the British ruled over us. These are the Fundamental Rights—Article 14 through to Article 32—that we have given ourselves as a free people. It is an essential difference that separates the system of governance after Independence from what came before it under the various rules and rulers India went through.

Fundamental Rights are those that have a high degree of protection from the encroachment of the State. These did not exist for us as a subject people; we gave these rights to ourselves as an independent nation made up of free citizens.

Part 1 of the Constitution (Articles 1–4) defines the Union and its territory.
Part 2 (Article 5–13) defines citizenship.
Part 3 is about Fundamental Rights, showing how important they are.
Article 12 defines the entity we are discussing in this chapter ('the State includes the Government and Parliament of India and the Government and the Legislature of each of the States and all local or other authorities within the territory of India or under the control of the Government of India').
Article 13 defines what a law is ('any Ordinance, order, bye-law, rule, regulation, notification, custom or usage having in the territory of India the force of law').

Our Fundamental Rights are those through which we are assured equality, freedom from discrimination, the right to free speech, free association and free assembly, the right to life and liberty and the right to occupation, the right to education, the freedom to propagate, practice and manage religion and the freedom to move the Supreme Court if our Fundamental Rights are wrongly encroached or violated by the State.

This set of rights appears to be potent. But do we actually possess them? The answer is no. We are not entirely free.

Let us look at how easily the State has trespassed on rights we thought had a high degree of protection from encroachment:

Rule: Article 14, the first one, promises equality before law. It reads: 'The State shall not deny to any person equality before the law or the equal protection of the laws within the territory of India.'

Reality: Does it deliver? No. For example, India has passed a law that says the Muslim, Jew or atheist refugee from Afghanistan, Bangladesh and Pakistan who has entered India before 31 December 2014 will not be granted automatic citizenship—but the Hindu, Parsi, Sikh, Jain, Buddhist or Christian will be. Note that Article 14 guarantees equality without exception to 'any person' and not just any citizen. But the Indian State legislates in discriminatory fashion against some of us.[10]

Rule: Article 15 prohibits discrimination. It reads: 'The State shall not discriminate against any citizen on grounds only of religion, race, caste, sex, place of birth or any of them.'

Reality: A Dalit who converts to Christianity is discriminated by the State[11] and deprived of her right to reservation merely because of a change in her religion. Even though she may continue in the profession or trade that is seen as 'unclean' and affects her standing in society, she is denied her rights by the State. What makes this discrimination more apparent is that this same Fundamental Right authorizes the State to provide reservation for the weaker classes. This chiefly includes the Dalits, but they can be immediately seen as undeserving the moment they choose to believe in a particular god instead of the ones the State wants them to.

Rule: Article 16 guarantees equality of opportunity in employment by the State. It reads: 'There shall be equality of opportunity for all citizens in matters relating to employment or appointment to any office under the State' and that 'no citizen shall, on grounds only of religion, race, caste, sex, descent, place of birth, residence or any of them, be ineligible for, or discriminated against in respect of, any employment or office under the State.'

Reality: The Indian State discourages the hiring of Muslims in security agencies such as the Research and Analysis Wing. An *Outlook* article quoting former Research and Analysis Wing (R&AW) chief A.S. Dulat confirmed that this was indeed the case.[12]

Rule: Article 17 abolishes untouchability. It reads, '"Untouchability" is abolished and its practice in any form is forbidden. The enforcement of any disability arising out of "Untouchability" shall be an offence punishable in accordance with law.'

Reality: Does it deliver? The people to ask here would be the Dalit community. Their own experience in the State offering protection to them is poor.[13] Even laws written specifically to shield them from social discrimination, like the Scheduled Castes and Scheduled Tribes (Prevention of Atrocities) Act, are often and perhaps even mostly observed in their breach. Discrimination cases that Dalits file are often not registered.[14]

(Article 18 deals with the abolition of titles received from foreign countries.)

Rule: Article 19 is an umbrella Fundamental Right on freedom of speech, assembly, association, movement and profession. It reads:

All citizens shall have the right to:
- freedom of speech and expression
- assemble peaceably and without arms
- form associations or unions
- move freely throughout the territory of India
- reside and settle in any part of the territory of India
- practise any profession, or to carry on any occupation, trade or business

Reality: The Article delivers none of these rights to us.

India's first constitutional amendment restricts these Rights by qualifying them. Meaning that the State was given the authority to curb them through so-called 'reasonable restrictions.' Free speech, for instance, can be controlled by 'reasonable restrictions ... in the interests of the sovereignty and integrity of India, the security of the State, friendly relations with foreign States, public order, decency or morality, or in relation to contempt of court, defamation or incitement to an offence.'

The State can make any legislation it sees fit along the lines above, which are so broad as to fit anything into them.

Let's see the multiple ways the government has infringed upon the rights within Article 19.

Blocked

The Right of Indians to assemble peacefully has been blocked by both law and process. Citizens do not really have this right to peaceful assembly. They have the right to seek police permission to assemble peacefully. The police have the right to approve, deny or not reply (which is often the tactic used by the State in India, so that there is deniability). Assembly in the absence of written permission is treated as a violation of the law. Readers will be familiar with Section 144 of the Criminal Procedure Code which gives the State the right to arrest people engaged in 'unlawful assembly.'

Severely limited

The Right to form associations and unions is severely limited by the process of registration. The State can deny (or delay) registration of organizations it doesn't like. It can ban those it has a problem with. Again, overbroad laws that empower the State to define individuals as 'terrorists' without conviction or trial are used to hinder and restrict the Right to association.[15]

Non-existent

The Right to move freely across India doesn't exist for those visiting the Northeast. The Right to reside and settle in any part of the territory of India doesn't apply to Gujarat's Muslims because of a law particular to that state, as we will see.

Denied

The Right to practise any profession doesn't apply to butchers who have been told by the State that they cannot slaughter livestock, explicitly denying them their Fundamental Right.[16]

Article 19 gives freedom in its text only to entirely remove this freedom through its footnotes.

Rule: Article 20 is on convictions and says, among other things, that no person shall be compelled to be a witness against themselves.

Reality: Does it deliver? No. It is regularly flouted in India's terror laws, such as Terrorist and Disruptive Activities (Prevention) Act (TADA) and Prevention of Terrorism Act (POTA), 2002. The State uses torture and threats to extract confessions which are used as part of the evidence so frequently as to make this Right more or less absent.[17] Reiterating this, in April 2021, Chief Justice of India

N.V. Ramana pointed out that the threat to human rights and bodily integrity is the 'highest in police stations'.[18]

Rule: Article 21 says 'no person shall be deprived of his life or personal liberty except according to procedure established by law.'

Reality: It would not be absurd to ask whether this law is followed at all. Arrests and detention by the State in India are done usually through a breach of procedure. Torture by the police and custodial deaths are so regular as not to merit even front-page coverage.[19]

The 2020 annual report from the National Campaign Against Torture, a platform for non-profit organizations, revealed that 1,723 people were killed in custody between January 2019 and December 2019. This means five people were being killed in India every day in custody, and this was according to the National Human Rights Commission's official data.[20]

A National Crime Records Bureau report shows that between from 2005 and 2018, not a single policeman was convicted with respect to the death of five hundred persons remanded in police custody by courts.[21]

Rule: Article 22 says the State cannot arrest an individual without informing them of the case and giving them the right to consult a lawyer of their choice. Those arrested must be produced before a magistrate within 24 hours. This is standard text for most democracies and readers will be familiar with the Miranda warning ('you have the right to remain silent, you have the right to an attorney') which is often heard in American movies and shows.

Reality: The sting in Article 22 is in its tail which says that all this shall not apply 'to any person who is arrested or detained under any law providing for preventive detention.' This addition has legitimized preventive or administrative detention.

It will interest readers to know that there was a similar law in the Raj which allowed the British to jail Indians without charge or trial. It was called the Rowlatt Act, and Indians protested against it on 13 April 1919 at a place called Jallianwala Bagh in Amritsar. Today, there are Rowlatt Acts in each state which are used more frequently against Indians than during the Raj.[22]

(Article 23 is the Right against exploitation and makes human trafficking and forced labour illegal.)

(Article 24 is on the prohibition of employment of children, a Right that millions of Indian children will be surprised to know that they have.)

Rule: Article 25 gives Indians the Right to freely profess, practise and propagate religion.

Reality: Does it deliver? This, unfortunately, is not true. India's legislatures and courts have hacked away at this Right[23] over the years. The word 'propagate' had been included in this Right quite specifically at the insistence of India's Christians who saw proselytization as an article of their faith. The Constituent Assembly debates show this quite clearly. In time, India's state legislatures, then its high courts and finally the Supreme Court have removed the right to propagate quite comprehensively.[24] Indeed, in many states, even the right to profess and practise religion has been banned. Adults are required to apply for State permission to change their faith, give reasons for why they are doing so, share details of their income, place of residence, their caste, the names and addresses of those attending their conversion ceremony—see the author's previous work, *Our Hindu Rashtra*, for more details on this.[25]

Almost nobody is happy with the way this Right has evolved. Its footnotes give the State the power to regulate the financial aspects of religions. This has given the opportunity to several states to bring

under their control wealthy temple trusts, such as Siddhivinayak in Maharashtra, Tirupati in Andhra Pradesh and Sabarimala in Kerala, upsetting Hindu conservatives.[26]

Rule: Article 26 gives all religions the Right to manage their own affairs in matters of religion.

Reality: This is quite clearly violated by the intrusion of the State into the functioning of temples, as seen above. It also has been violated by the State intruding into the personal law of Muslims.[27]

Rule: Article 27 says citizens cannot be compelled to pay taxes whose proceeds are used for religious purposes.

Reality: This Right is violated by the State which spends money on pilgrimages like Haj, and constitutionally (through Article 290A) gives ₹46.5 lakh to the Kerala Devaswom Board and ₹13.5 lakh to the Tamil Nadu Devaswom Fund. But the State uses it wherever convenient to suppress citizens' rights. The Gujarat government used Article 27 as its defence when it refused to rebuild Muslim places of worship damaged in the 2002 riots.[28]

Rule: Article 28 says no schools run by the State shall provide religious instruction.

Reality: In 2017, the Madras High Court made the recitation of 'Vande Mataram' compulsory in schools once a week (and more bizarrely, in government and private offices once a month). Chhattisgarh made it compulsory in schools a few years before that and other states, including Telangana, have tried imposing it. The justification given is that this is not a religious verse though it includes praying to an anthropomorphic image that many feel uncomfortable doing.

To think that just three decades earlier, Kerala resident Bijoe Emmanuel had challenged the Department of Education for suspending his children on the ground that they refused to recite the national anthem during the morning assemblies. In a landmark ruling for free speech in India, the Supreme Court said, 'there is no provisions of law which obliges anyone to sing the National Anthem.'[29]

Rule: Article 29 gives citizens the Right to conserve their language, script and culture. And it says, 'no citizen shall be denied admission into any educational institution maintained by the State or receiving aid out of State funds on grounds only of religion, race, caste, language or any of them.'

Reality: This Right becomes hollow when, as we have noted, the State runs Urdu schools through teachers who do not know how to read or write Urdu.[30]

Rule: Article 30 gives India's minorities, whether based on religion or language, the Right to 'establish and administer educational institutions of their choice.' The State has been intruding here as well. In 2020 the West Bengal government took away (and the Supreme Court approved) the right of madrasas to appoint teachers.[31]

Reality: This is another Right that nobody is really happy with. Hindu groups believe that the exclusion of minority institutions, whether linguistic or religious, from the Right to Education Act's provisions for 25 per cent reservations for the poor, make their schools uncompetitive against those run by Christian groups.

(Article 31 was originally about the Right to property (which was abolished) and now deals with the acquisition of property by the State.)

Rule: Article 32 is the Right to move the Supreme Court for enforcement of Fundamental Rights.

Reality: This has turned out to be mostly useless for those violations which the State has an interest in continuing. For example, habeas corpus matters in which those detained in Kashmir demand their right to be produced and heard in court are kicked down the road so regularly as to make the Right abolished.[32]

This is the state of our Fundamental Rights. The Constitution resembles a Potemkin village. A facade that looks substantial but behind which there is little or nothing. The State's intrusion into our Rights is as crude and as it is persistent. The qualifications (reasonable restrictions which are for the most part extremely unreasonable) to the Rights violate the universalism and beauty of the Indian Constitution and what it promises, which is a better, more just and freer world for all of us.

The problem here, once again as it is with the engagement with the State on other matters, is that the most influential set of Indians (us) are for the most part disengaged from the substance. The State has a free run to continue in the manner that it has been from the start. The Nehruvian state, if we can call the structure that emerged

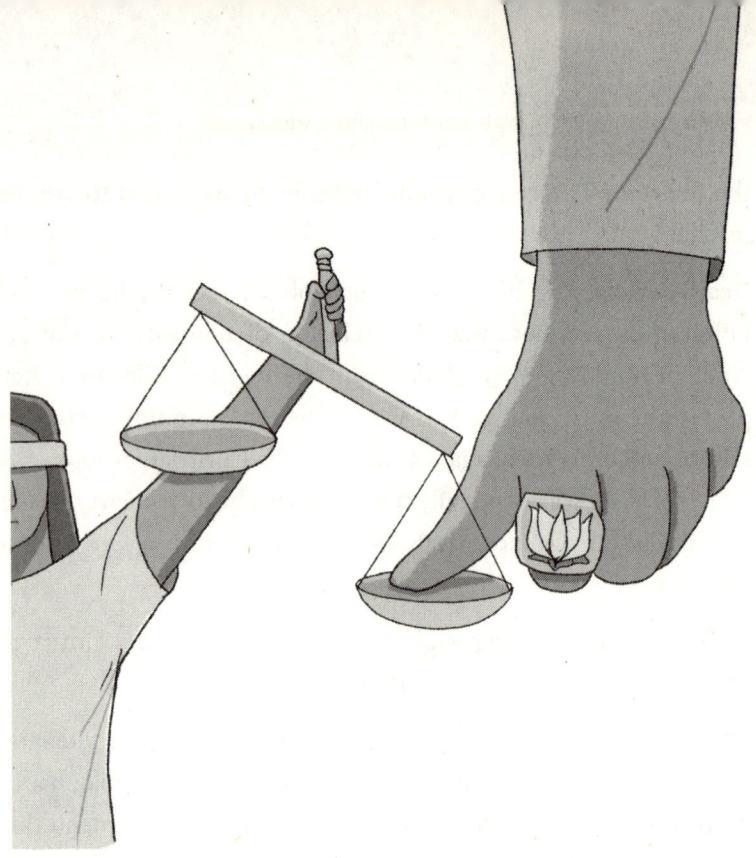

in August 1947, and has continued till our times, is a State for elites, first the colony's occupier and now the political and upper class. The political class needs to make the laws harsh and remove the freedoms so that it can rule more efficiently while denying freedoms. The upper class has almost no investment in the State's functioning, either on the side of delivery or that of the criminal justice system and other freedoms, so it is happy to let things slide. This is the state of affairs that we have had from the start and has continued till recent times.

But while things have never really been good in India in terms of civil liberties and individual freedoms, there has been a sharp deterioration and acceleration away from Rights in recent times. The State has deliberately demoted individual freedoms and Fundamental Rights and appropriated more power for itself.

This is authoritarianism. The dictionary defines being authoritarian as 'enforcing strict obedience to authority at the expense of personal freedom' and 'showing a lack of concern for the wishes or opinions of others.' Is it the case that we have entered a period of authoritarianism in India and, if so, how can we show it to be the case?

3

At the Edge of Autocracy

Most of us, and especially the media, may not be looking at how the State in India functions on issues of freedom, but there are groups around the world that regularly monitor such things. And their findings over the last few years do not make for good reading if you are an Indian.

India in 2020 slipped to its lowest-ever position on an index released by The Economist Intelligence Unit (EIU). From twenty-seven in 2014, it fell twenty-four places to be ranked fifty-one.[33] The EIU, run by the conservative and highly respected *Economist* magazine, measured sixty indicators including electoral process and pluralism, civil liberties, government functioning, political participation and political culture. It classifies nations as having one of four types of regime: full democracy, flawed democracy, hybrid regime and authoritarian regime.

The EIU classified India as a flawed democracy.

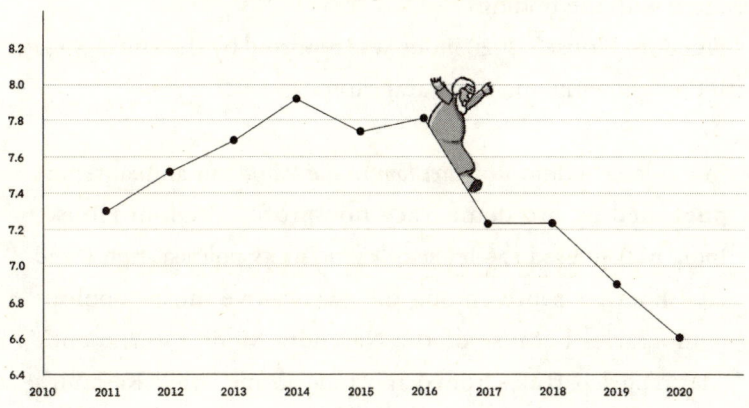

EIU Democracy Index: India

India has plummeted in global freedom indices across several sectors, including in those where it was never particularly good in the first place. Take, for instance, Reporters Without Borders' World Press Freedom Index which measures pluralism, media independence and transparency, among other things. In 2021, India was ranked 142 in the world.[34]

Another monitoring organization is Freedom House, founded in 1941 in the United States (US) to champion the advancement of freedom globally. Over the decades, it has recorded the way in which countries have performed on the issues of democracy and human rights. It has been criticized by many for its approach during the Cold War, but its recent critics are usually states like Russia and China.

According to Freedom House's *Freedom in the World Report* for 2021,[35] India first managed to sink Kashmir's status from 'Partly Free' previously to 'Not Free' after gutting Article 370 in 2019, locking up its leaders, and denying the entire population access to the Internet.

Anyone familiar with the position in that region will find it hard to disagree with the finding.

Freedom House's 2020 index was reported by the *Huffington Post* with the following opening paragraphs:

> In the latest edition of *Freedom in the World*, an annual report published by pro-democracy non-profit Freedom House, India has suffered the largest decline in its political rights and civil liberties score among the twenty-five most populous democracies because of the Narendra Modi government's 'alarming departures from democratic norms', while Kashmir's status has declined from 'Partly Free' to 'Not Free'.
>
> This 2020 report gives a damning assessment of the Modi government's 'pattern of Hindu nationalist policies', including the persecution of religious minorities, abruptly revoking Jammu and Kashmir's autonomy, the adoption of the Citizenship Amendment Act (CAA), which it calls a 'discriminatory citizenship law', and the 'aggressive' suppression of the anti-CAA protests that followed.[36]

In 2021, Freedom House rated India as being 'partly free.' The reasons cited included:

> The fall of India from the upper ranks of free nations could have a particularly damaging impact on global democratic standards. Political rights and civil liberties in the country have deteriorated since Narendra Modi became prime minister in 2014, with increased pressure on human rights organizations, rising intimidation of academics and journalists, and a spate of bigoted attacks, including lynchings, aimed at Muslims. The decline only accelerated after Modi's re-election in 2019 ... The government of

Prime Minister Narendra Modi and its state-level allies continued to crack down on critics during the year, and their response to Covid-19 included a ham-fisted lockdown that resulted in the dangerous and unplanned displacement of millions of internal migrant workers. The ruling Hindu nationalist movement also encouraged the scapegoating of Muslims, who were disproportionately blamed for the spread of the virus and faced attacks by vigilante mobs. Rather than serving as a champion of democratic practice and a counterweight to authoritarian influence from countries such as China, Modi and his party are tragically driving India itself toward authoritarianism.[37]

The World Justice Project's Rule of Law Index, which looks at Fundamental Rights, the justice system, restraint on government power and so on, ranked India at sixty-nine in 2020, down from fifty-nine in 2015.[38] (For more details on over thirty such indicators and India's position on them, see the author's work *Price of the Modi Years*.)[39]

To understand what is going on with the numbers that are pointing to a decline in India's civil liberties and other freedoms, let us examine one index in some detail.

CIVICUS, established in 1993 and headquartered in Johannesburg, is an association of civil society organizations with 9,000 members around the world. It monitors the state of civil liberties in 193 nations around the world and, through the input of data, grades them as being either open, narrowed, obstructed, repressed or closed.

Broadly, the definitions of CIVICUS were as follows:

Open: Civil spaces enjoyed freely by all. There are low levels of fear, there is freedom to form associations and demonstrate in public, freedom to spread and receive information without restrictions.

The authorities are tolerant to criticism and willing to engage with civil society. Police protection is given to protesters, there is free speech that adheres to international standards and a free media and uncensored online content.

Countries that make the cut: 'Open' nations included Canada, Uruguay and Suriname in the Americas, Taiwan and New Zealand in Asia and Germany, Finland, Norway, Sweden, Switzerland and Ireland in Europe.

Narrowed: The State allows civil society and individuals to exercise rights to free speech, association, assembly and expression but violations of these also occur. Enjoyment of rights is impeded by harassment, arrest and assault. Protests are allowed but sometimes impeded and denied permission. Media is free but influenced by the State.

Countries that make the cut: Nations with 'narrowed' civic spaces were more spread across the world. These included the US, France, the United Kingdom (UK), Italy, South Africa, Botswana, Argentina, Namibia, Ghana, Chile, Japan and South Korea.

Obstructed: Here, the civic space is limited. Though civil society organizations exist, the State harasses them through illegal surveillance, bureaucratic harassment and demeaning public statements. Citizens can assemble peacefully but are vulnerable to excessive use of force. There is some space for editorial independence, but journalists face criminal defamation laws and physical attacks, encouraging self-censorship.

Countries that make the cut: India was ranked 'obstructed' along with Brazil, Kenya, Kazakhstan, Nepal, Mongolia, Morocco, Ukraine, Sri Lanka, Indonesia, Zambia, Mozambique and the Philippines.

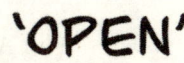

On 4 December 2019, CIVICUS downgraded India from 'obstructed' to 'repressed'.[40] Clubbed with nations such as Pakistan, Afghanistan, Sudan, Algeria, Russia and Myanmar, India's new rating meant that democratic freedoms—such as the freedoms of expression, peaceful assembly and association—were significantly constrained by the State. The rating changed after a year of thorough assessment of the state of civic freedoms in the country—the Indian government's lockdown and internet blackout in Jammu and Kashmir and its actions against students, journalists and human rights activists. The government's stated hostility to human rights non-governmental organizations (NGOs) was mentioned in the press release announcing the downgrading. It referred to raids on groups such as Lawyers Collective, Amnesty International India and Greenpeace India.

To understand why India was downgraded, let us see the exact definition CIVICUS applies here. It defines a repressed space thus:

> Civic space is significantly constrained. Active individuals and civil society members who criticize power holders risk surveillance, harassment, intimidation, imprisonment, injury and death. Although some civil society organizations exist, their advocacy work is regularly impeded and they face threats of de-registration and closure by the authorities. People who organize or take part in peaceful protests are likely to be targeted by the authorities through the use of excessive force, including the use of live ammunition, and risk mass arrests and detention. The media typically reflects the position of the state, and any independent voices are routinely targeted through raids, physical attacks or protracted legal harassment. Websites and social media platforms are blocked and internet activism is heavily monitored.[41]

This is a textbook definition of India as it is today. The six questions CIVICUS asks that we must answer are:

1. Are active individuals and groups who criticize the Indian government's policies harassed?
2. Is the work of Indian civil society groups regularly impeded and are they threatened with deregistration and closure?
3. Are peaceful protesters targeted in India?
4. Does the Indian media reflect the position of the State?
5. Are individual voices harassed here?
6. Are social media platforms blocked and is internet activism monitored in India?

Let's take it point by point:

Are active individuals and groups who criticize the Indian government's policies harassed?

Yes. The list of individuals and groups active in the civic space who criticize the Indian government and are being harassed is long. It includes the Centre for Justice and Peace—run by Teesta Setalvad, who has for many years tried to find justice for the Gujarat riots—which was raided by the Central Bureau of Investigation (CBI) in July 2015;[42] Lawyers Collective, the activist group working on transgender rights and decriminalization of homosexuality, raided by the CBI in July 2019;[43] Amnesty International India, working on human rights, raided by the Enforcement Directorate (ED) in October 2018 and the CBI in November 2019;[44] Greenpeace India, working on environmental rights, raided by the ED in October 2018;[45] Navsarjan Trust, working on Dalit rights and manual scavenging has had its funding cut off and licence taken away;[46]

similarly, Act Now for Harmony and Democracy (ANHAD), which combats communalism, and Indian Social Action Forum (INSAF) have been harassed.[47]

These are only the prominent names. Many of these groups have a global reputation (Amnesty International, where the author worked till 2019, won the Nobel Peace Prize in 1977). The Indian government has had to manage the international fallout of this, with concerns raised by the International Commission of Jurists, the United Nation's Special Rapporteurs, the European Union and other global bodies.

Is the work of Indian civil society groups regularly impeded and are they threatened with deregistration and closure?

Yes. The State has either launched criminal action against, frozen the accounts of, blocked the funding to and generally prevented the functioning of thousands of civil society organizations and individuals. In the three years between March 2017 and March 2020, the government deregistered more than six thousand organizations.[48] Most of these organizations, about 70 per cent of them, worked in the education sector, the State said. A November 2017 report by CIVICUS stated that the Indian government cancelled the registration of 4,470 organizations between 5 May and 9 June 2015.[49] On 28 April 2015, *Hindustan Times* reported that 8,975 organizations had been deregistered.[50] On 4 December 2019, *Business Standard* reported that the government has banned 14,500 NGOs under the FCRA Act from receiving foreign funds, and that the Modi government, in its first term, had aggressively gone after civil society organizations to try and shut them down.[51]

Foreign Contribution (Regulation) Act (FCRA) refers to a law used to regulate foreign contributions to Indian organizations. India welcomes foreign investment in manufacturing bombs, guns, alcohol and cigarettes but rebuffs it in education, health and rights. FCRA was legislated to stop funding in Indian politics but has been turned around to target NGOs. (To know more, see p. xx.)

Are peaceful protesters targeted in India?

Yes. The State in India has always criminalized protest, but this has been turbo-charged in recent years. Not only are protesters harassed but they are persecuted and victimized. The government has loaded absurd charges on to those who dissent to keep them in jail. To give one example, the Allahabad High Court released Dr Kafeel Khan, who was jailed under the National Security Act for a peaceful protest, saying that his detention had been illegal.[52] The Union government has jailed under terror laws student protesters like Umar Khalid, who has no record of either criminal action or incitement (which he has been falsely accused of). Similarly, activists such as Sudha Bharadwaj (a lawyer who gave up her US citizenship to work in India), eighty-year-old poet and academic Varavara Rao (given bail on medical grounds), human rights advocates Arun Ferreira and Surendra Gadling, English professor Shoma Sen and activist Rona Wilson refused bail because they were charged with absolutely no evidence under the anti-terror law Unlawful Activities (Prevention) Act.[53] They were arrested after a celebratory gathering by Dalits in Bhima Koregaon in Maharashtra was attacked by a Hindutva mob, even though some of them were not even present there.[54] This is a circumstance similar to the violence provoked in Delhi which was used to arrest those not present.

Does the Indian media reflect the position of the State?

For the most part, yes. The media in India is diverse in terms of its forms, with television, print and online all being represented, in terms of its linguistic spread and in terms of its ideological bent. But the fact is that the largest media houses are aligned with the government. One reason is that the government is by far the largest advertiser in India (the Union government alone spent almost ₹1,700 crore on advertisements in print and electronic media between 2018 and 2021;[55] it has discretionary power over this spend). The media houses are dependent on this not just for profitability but for survival.

The second reason is that the government actively harasses organizations that are seen as dissenting. For example, NDTV and Raghav Bahl's *Network 18* (before he had to sell to Reliance) have been marked out and acted against, whether in terms of cases or denial of licences.[56]

A third reason is that many media houses are aligned with the majoritarian agenda of the State and enthusiastically support the harassment and bullying of minorities.[57]

Are individual voices harassed here?

Yes. Individual voices, and especially those that are prominent, are harassed in India. Deepika Padukone stood, without speaking, at an event in Jawaharlal Nehru University on 7 January 2020 to protest against the violence unleashed by the ABVP against its students. She was humiliated[58] and dragged recklessly into the absurd case concerning the suicide of the actor Sushant Singh Rajput. Aamir Khan has faced hostility for noticing that the climate in India has become intolerant.[59] The activist Harsh Mander and the scholar Yogendra Yadav were dragged into the Delhi riots case purely because the government doesn't like what they say.[60]

Are social media platforms blocked and is internet activism monitored in India?

Yes. India routinely asks social media platforms to block individuals and delete content. In the six months between July and December 2019, Twitter was asked by the Indian government 789 times to take some action.[61] The author's own Twitter account was withheld after a tweet on protest in June 2020. It has been reported that India conducts mass surveillance of its citizens and social media activities.[62]

In July 2021, an investigation by seventeen media organizations around the world, supported by Amnesty Tech, found that a software called Pegasus had been used to spy on Opposition leaders, political strategists and tacticians, journalists, activists, minority leaders, Supreme Court judges, religious leaders, union ministers, the army, the election commissioners and the CBI. The spy software, costing millions of dollars, was licenced from an Israeli firm which only has governments as its clients.

The government of India did not deny using the software but chose to block an investigation into it.[63] Even parliamentary scrutiny was disallowed, and bureaucrats were ordered not to appear before parliamentary subcommittees on the issues. The Supreme Court then ordered a committee to examine the issue in October 2021.

It is easy to conclude that the ranking CIVICUS has given India—as being a 'repressed' place—is dead accurate by definition.

We, as a nation, are actually not too far from being consigned to the very end of the spectrum, as a society that is 'closed'. CIVICUS defines this as:

> There is complete closure—in law and in practice—of civic space. An atmosphere of fear and violence prevails, where state and powerful non-state actors are routinely allowed to imprison, seriously injure and kill people with impunity for attempting to exercise their rights to associate, peacefully assemble and express themselves. Any criticism of the ruling authorities is severely punished and there is virtually no media freedom. The internet is heavily censored, many websites are blocked and online criticism of power holders is subject to severe penalties.[64]

As of 2021, China, Vietnam, Iran, Egypt and Saudi Arabia have been listed as 'closed'. The elements that define this rating are:

- No civic space for individuals and groups to engage in democratic dissent
- Fear of the State
- Routine jailing of individuals, lynchings and gratuitous violence against protesters

- Little media freedom
- Restricted and censored internet where dissent is criminalized

All of these things are applicable to large parts of India already, including Kashmir, which is why Freedom House marks it as being 'not free'.[65] Chhattisgarh and other parts of the Adivasi belt and states in the Northeast have a similar situation.

Governments in India are democratically elected, or at least they are in most parts (Kashmir has no elections and is under Central rule and military occupation). That gives us the impression that it is free society. But the right to elect individuals is only one measure of freedom. The true test is the enjoyment of Constitutional Rights. Here, India has failed. The space for civil society is shrinking even in those parts where things were thought to be normal.

In 2020, the Indian government introduced changes to the law which would make running NGOs next to impossible. Their continuation would be at the mercy of the State. *Scroll* reported that the changes 'will have far-reaching consequences on the fields of education, health, people's livelihoods, gender justice and indeed democracy in India'.[66]

These words must be taken seriously. We need not be told by the media that such arbitrary actions damage us as a society in many ways. This is not about NGOs or those who they work for, it is about society at large.

The world has noticed a deterioration of the conditions in India. Two sets of questions arise from this. The first set is: How can this slide be first paused and then reversed? And who will do this?

4

The Crumbling Pillars of Democracy

Let us look at the possibilities.

There appear to be four places where enough power resides for the conditions to be changed.

The first is the State itself, which can look at what it has done and what it is doing and choose to reverse course.

The second is the Opposition, which, in a democracy, is the group tasked with opposing laws and policies they disagree with and can bring about change democratically.

The third is the judiciary, which is responsible for checking executive overreach and ensuring the rule of Constitutionalism.

The fourth is the external world, those multilateral bodies that India is a part of and whose opinion it values.

Let us have a look at each of these in turn. The government is not a monolith. It comprises individuals from different parts of the country, some of whom may or may not share the desire of other people to carry on or increase the repression of civil liberties. The government is also a partnership of one major party with other regional parties which may not agree with the ideological aspects and be able to influence change. Then the government or the State is essentially the political force plus the machinery which comprises bureaucrats, diplomats and policemen of high rank. They are not all of the same background or of the same mindset and could put forth their opposition to the things being done.

All of the things above are true. It is also true that India is being led by an individual who is popular and whose popularity has given him political capital. This is not easy to resist from within, even assuming there is some element of disagreement at the level of the party, with allies or with individuals charged with running government functions. The charismatic and popular leader, especially one with certitude and the desire to bring about quick and sweeping change, is not easy to push back against. This is particularly so in our part of the world where internal dissent is no different from treason. It is possible, but not easy, to expect and believe that the State will change its behaviour voluntarily for these reasons. In any case, the experience of several years under this government and the direction it has taken the State and nation in should give an indication of what is realistically possible.

The answer is: Not much.

The Opposition in India is said to be weak and incompetent. Whether or not that is true is not as material to our examination as is the question of whether it is invested in the issue in oppositional terms. The fact is that it is not, to a large extent. The next section will show in more detail why this is the case. Democratic politics is about the capture of power first. In India, the way the Opposition exerts itself is through popular issues. These include such things as the rights of farmers and the rights of large groups claiming reservation. Parties in the Opposition are often enthusiastic about joining in and throwing their weight behind them because there is the expectation of political reward.

Civil rights and individual liberties, on the other hand, are not the sort of issues that have been in the domain of mainstream politics in India. One reason, as we have seen, is that the most influential and vocal part of the society (us) is not especially concerned about it. The other is that even where there is a large group willing to resist the State's actions, such as the nationwide protests against the citizenship laws in 2019 and early 2020, the Opposition is unwilling to join in for fear that it will be seen as supporting Indians of a particular religion, in this instance, Muslims.

The BJP has been successful in inverting the idea of communal politics and those demanding legitimate constitutional rights are seen as anti-national purely because of their religion, which is not that of the majority. There are parts of the Opposition that have ideologically stood against the erosion of civil rights, but these parties and their voices are small and weak when ranged against the behemoth of the Indian State being controlled by a strong party.

The judiciary has historically been the protector of rights in democracies when it comes to stopping the executive from damaging the State and victimizing citizens. But the judiciary can only do so in two ways. The first is through individual cases that come up before it or those it chooses to take up itself ('suo moto'). This is episodic and not systemic. The judiciary can undo some of the damage that the State is doing in individual cases, such as that of Dr Kafeel Khan, and give justice, but this is rare.

Justice moves slowly in India. Justice is also subject to the law and the law itself is the problem in many instances, as we will see later in this book. The last reason why the judiciary may not be the ideal ally of those wanting a freer India is that it has a history of succumbing to the strong leader. The Supreme Court validated the 1975 Emergency of Indira Gandhi and allowed her to suspend Fundamental Rights. It has a history of siding with the State against the citizen when forced to choose. It is not always in reality what it promises to be on paper.

The last actor here is the external world. Here the answer is that it is the most active of all the players in trying to get India to do the right thing. Why? Because the world has respect for India, the largest democracy on the planet and many nations and multilateral bodies that we are participants in and members of expect the Indian State to do better with our own citizens that it has. But the world's bodies have limited influence on a State, particularly when the State is itself invested strongly in the idea, as is the case in India today, of an iron fist against its citizens. If the issue had been one which the State did not care much about, foreign influence would have worked effectively. It still does work: One reason why the Citizenship Amendment Act (CAA) was legislated but not actually enacted was because of external pressure. This made the Modi government reluctant to notify its rules, thus delaying its application. And so external pressure works, but in limited fashion.

Just like the ruling party and government itself, the Opposition, the judiciary and the outside world, we must expect neither self-correction nor a pause or halt brought about externally to the shrinking of civic space. We must, however, expect that they will each contribute in some manner, even if very small, to change if there is sufficient pressure. They are all important and but none by itself can make the difference. The element that is required in our society is the one that most mature democracies have but is missing to a large extent in ours—the participation of individuals in democracy beyond the electoral process.

Let us now turn to the second set of questions. These have to do with something even more basic. Why exactly is the State attempting to suppress freedoms, when it is clear that India has a dominant political force and a popular leader? Surely it is not for political power, which is already in the possession of the ruling party. Our attention must turn to what dissenting groups and individuals of civil society are asking for which is so objectionable as to be attacked in this fashion. What changes do they want? Why are they protesting? Why are they associating? Why are they assembling? What laws are they objecting to?

This is the subject of our next chapter.

Informed dissent makes democracy better.

It makes it more efficient at what it is ultimately meant to do—raise the standards of living of its people, give them more freedom to express themselves, give individuals more space to live the sort of lives they want to without interference and produce a society that lives in harmony and prosperity and equality.

This book, then, will tell you why you should dissent and protest against the injustices of the State against individuals. And how.

5

Beginning Your Activism Journey

If there is one pressing point that this work seeks to make, it is this: The situation is serious, and it requires all individuals in India to stand up for constitutional rights, for human rights and for a progressive society. This we cannot leave as individuals to the political parties or to the electoral process as something that will sort itself out. The problem has emerged despite all of the above. It requires the time and attention and actions of us as individuals.

For you, it means it's time to embark on your activist journey. The steps to becoming an individual activist involve:

- Awareness
- Dissemination
- Widening the circle
- Identifying the Middle
- Calibrating the message
- Producing good content
- Collectivism

Fact: Activism is passion but under that is usually a layer of dispassionate knowledge which is the foundation.

Knowing the law and the facts are a foundational aspect and the most important element of activism. Most activists know and understand the laws better than the rest. Laws and their text are generally not read or understood by the many, including those who support or criticize them. But this is not always because the laws are complex to read.

The entire operative text of the Citizenship Amendment Act (CAA), which introduced for the first time religion into Indian citizenship, is just 624 words. It separates 'illegal migrants' coming to India from three nations by the faith they were born into and lists six religions that are welcome. By implication, the law then isolates the one that is unwelcome. This is in violation of Article 14 of India's Constitution, which gives all persons in India equality before the law and equal protection of the laws. If there are two migrants of different faiths, and the religion of only one of them is on the list of six identified in the CAA, then the other is being denied equality by the State which is a breach of that individual's Fundamental Rights.

India's Constitution cannot be broken by a law. That is why CAA has to be opposed and that is how an activist would understand the issue.

The other thing that activists understand and know better than the rest is the facts. And the reason they do is because they have enough interest in a subject to dig into it more than the rest.

Awareness of an issue and its facts, by itself, is the most powerful weapon of activism. Think about it—if all of us were aware of the objective reality, our disputes would be few. The points of difference would be quite limited because both sides would know and agree on the facts. Only the perspective would differ. That, however, is not the case in reality.

Many of us are agitated over something that we do not fully understand but think we do. It would help us to encounter someone who informs us about the facts, especially if they do so in a way that appears to be non-confrontational and rational. This is key. Activism is passion but under that is usually a layer of dispassionate knowledge which is the foundation.

If you know the facts, you have taken the first step, the most important step as an activist. Let's go to the next step.

THE ACTIVIST BRAIN

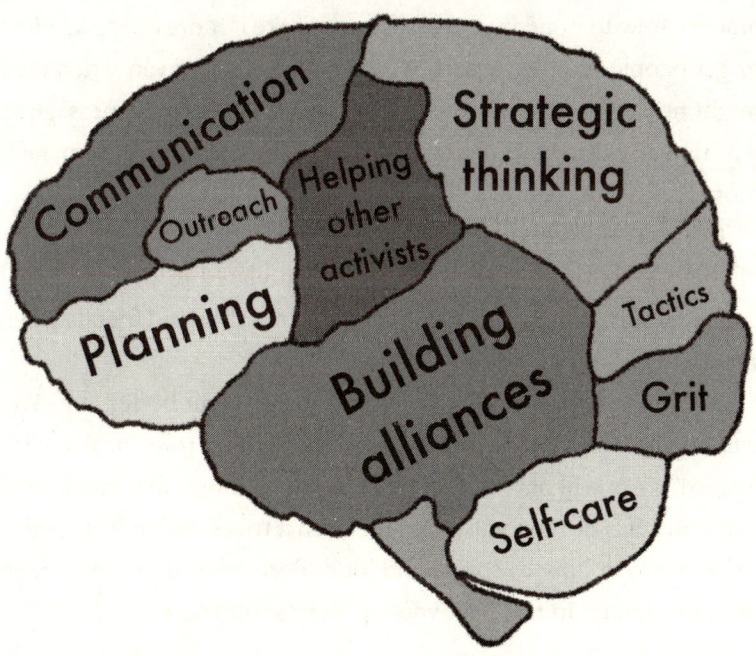

Fact: Knowing the facts is useful only if one is able to propagate them.

This is the second stage of becoming an activist. Here we have to consider three things. First, how can you widen the circle of those who know what you now do about an issue? Second, how do you engage with them? And third, how do you convince them to consider seeing things as you see them?

Of course, we all know that the first one is easy to answer. That is because we are already in touch with quite a few people regularly and exchanging material with them on social media. An excellent place to start your activism is on family groups. Family members will hold different views from yours but will be more willing to listen to what you have to say. And they will also give you the opportunity to practice how to hone your message and make it more effective. How to get people to engage with what you are saying even when they might not agree with it; how to craft and calibrate your message so that they are drawn to it; and what form to present it in to make it more likely that they will actually hear you.

Consider the fact that someone who does not usually post videos of themselves or does not post videos unrelated to their personal lives, will always draw the attention of her relatives and friends when she does so.

As you begin doing this, you will of course get better at it. You will begin to be more prepared when the camera rolls (or you click 'record'). You will have noted down the main things that you intend to say, in advance. You will have rehearsed it to see which words need to be stressed, how to sound and look more relaxed, or concerned or entertaining. In this way, you will very soon know

- how to engage your friends and relatives;

- how to engage with a broader circle (activists like to be connected and if you produce good content, you will join their circles!); and
- how to present facts and laws.

This will make you someone whose content others want to follow, retweet and forward. This, in turn, will help you be more invested in the things you are interested in.

Reclaiming our rights as free citizens will be the primary battle of Indian democracy. You may have read that the world sees India as only partially democratic. The electoral process, meaning the right of citizens to choose their legislators and the executive, is only half of democracy. The other half is the freedom and liberty that individual citizens have with respect to encroachment from the State, meaning the apparatus of government.

In India, over time and especially in recent years, what the State calls reasonable restrictions on the rights of citizens have overwhelmed the Fundamental Rights. The government has exerted itself against the citizen through the bureaucracy and the police, political leadership and the judiciary. The pushback from civil society that was present during the freedom movement under the Raj is being undermined and crushed under democracy.

The primary battle to be fought in India is the one against the State's appropriation of civil liberties and freedoms.

How do we carry out this struggle? We do so at the individual level, through awareness and through spreading the message of our rights and by standing in support of others.

This is what we will discuss in the next chapter: how you can plan your own campaign for change.

SECTION II

How to Cook

6

Are You Ready to Stir Things Up?

Activism is your right. It is one of your freedoms. It gives you agency and the power to influence authority.

Activism, writer Tim Gee tells us, puts power (kratia) in the people (demos), the Greek words that give us democracy. It tells us that democracy means more than the right to vote. Activism is something you're already doing now, by tweeting or writing a post about something you feel strongly about. To make it more effective, you need to make it targeted and focused. This book will try and help show you how.

Activists can be from any side of the political spectrum. In many democracies, activism is a part of the political process and concerns the supporters and members of all major parties. In America, there are activists that support the right of the woman to have an abortion (pro-choice) and activists that oppose this right (pro-life).

Activism of the modern age is also India's gift to the world.

Gee, an activist himself, says all civic protests use Gandhi as their template. So, protest is good and wholesome and deeply and truly Indian in the best way possible. Gandhi's opposition to the Raj was through a series of protests such as the Dandi march (resisting the British monopoly on salt), Champaran (against farmers forced to cultivate indigo), Kheda (against taxation on farmers in a time of famine) and non-cooperation movement (against sedition and other Raj laws).

Civil disobedience in Ghana brought it independence in 1957 from colonial rule. Non-violent revolutions produced freedom for Poland, Czechoslovakia, Estonia, Lithuania and Latvia in the 1980s. In the 2000s, too, such revolutions rule took place against autocratic regimes in Georgia, Ukraine and Serbia, as well as in Egypt and Tunisia.

Every one of these campaigns were informed by the principles applied by Gandhi and the Indians: an insistence on the truth (Satya-Agraha), and peaceful dissent.

Gandhi's belief was that even the most powerful cannot rule without the consent of the ruled.

We honour Gandhi and India's contribution to the world when we do even a little activism. Activism is a good word. And remember: The opposite of an Activist appears to be a 'Passivist'. Is that something you'd like to be?

(Note: Pacifism is the doctrine that disputes, especially those between countries, should be settled without recourse to violence. Passivism is the quality or principle of being passive.)

What counts as activism?

Activism is defined as the use of direct and noticeable action to achieve a result, usually a political or social one. It is defined by Wikipedia as individual or collective effort to 'promote, impede, direct, or intervene in social, political, economic, legal, or environmental reform with the desire to make changes in society toward a perceived greater good.' No change is possible without activism, and change is always the result of someone or something pushing the effort without which, as Newton's first law tells us, things continue as they are.

So, what is it that activists do? A range of things which we will discuss further in later chapters. It goes from just conversations with family and friends and spreading messages on social media to attending and speaking at public rallies, joining an affinity group, an NGO or a civil liberties group, and volunteering to work and organizing events.

A lot of things!

Quiz: Are You Ready to Activate Your Inner Activist?

The path to becoming socially responsible is not as difficult as you might think. First, find out where you stand:

Your building society has decided not to allow Muslims to occupy flats. What is your reaction?

1. You decide to move out.
2. Refuse to sign the minutes of the society meeting.
3. Start a petition to challenge this rule.
4. Ignore it. What do you care anyway?

While walking down the street, you see a person being harassed. You decide to

1. Whip out your phone and record the incident to post on social media.
2. Tell the person to stop and ask the victim if they are okay.
3. Find the nearest police station and report the incident.
4. Walk away.

At a party, you hear some comments made by a friend that you feel are inappropriate. You

1. Confront the microaggressions with harsh language.
2. Initiate a conversation to understand your friend's perspective.
3. Use this as an opportunity to educate your friend.
4. Brush aside this painful interaction.

What is more important to you?

1. The life of someone from the same social class.
2. The life of someone from a different social class.
3. They are both equally important.
4. My own life is the only one important to me.

What does the word 'privilege' mean to you?

1. An opportunity that gives me great pleasure.
2. People who have it easy in life.
3. People who are not minorities in certain cultures have various advantages in that society.
4. I have a right to certain benefits.

Answers

Mostly 1s: Congratulations! It's great to know you have the desire to do the right thing. Unfortunately, you've chosen the wrong way to go about it.

Mostly 2s: Your eyes are open to the many social and political injustices but you have an incomplete understanding of the problem.

Mostly 3s: You're aware of the many unfair and discriminating aspects of our society and are responding in a constructive way. Fight the good fight!

Mostly 4s: You're completely oblivious to what's going on around you. Please read this book.

7

The Not-So-Secret Sauce of Activism

Now it's time to consider the basics: How do organizations begin to build a campaign? They do so by first knowing that all large goals are reached by securing smaller, more manageable goals. It is the accretion of these smaller achievements that results in the final 'win'.

Naturally, these smaller goals and wins need to be aligned to the main objective. So how can we know if our smaller and more achievable targets are the right ones? That is what this chapter will tell you.

Theory of Change

Campaigning organizations and activists don't just show up at a protest with no preparation like sports fans (well, even sports fans often turn up prepared with banners, posters and songs). Activists understand that a rally or a petition is part of a larger plan for producing the result required. This plan is our recipe, which is called a Theory of Change. As the name suggests, it is a process which lays out how and why a change is possible and victory—meaning a shift in the rights position or situation—achievable.

Theory of Change identifies a long-term goal and then maps it backwards to figure out how to get there through specific steps.

This is how NGOs and even companies go about their work for social change.

This is how the Indian National Congress (INC) and Mahatma Gandhi planned the freedom struggle. It is how the African National Congress (ANC) and Nelson Mandela went about their struggle against institutionalized racism in South Africa.

The goal for INC's Theory of Change was independence from the British Raj. The goal for the ANC's Theory of Change was the end of Apartheid.

Theory of Change logically lays out the path to the goal through short-term, medium-term and long-term conditions that are created through activism. These conditions are called outcomes, which are the material consequences of activism. The outcomes framework determines the types of activities and interventions needed to achieve the ultimate goal.

And so the longer term goal is accomplished through the achievement of specific shorter-term outcomes. A cricket captain might understand this as breaking down a series of steps that takes his team to the 250-run target.

The outcomes pathway plots the creation of the circumstances under which difficult or longer-term change becomes more possible.

All large goals are achieved at the end of smaller, more manageable goals.

The way in which the INC finally won self-rule for India was through a series of steps in which it had already appropriated some aspects of self-rule. In the Indian elections, held in 1920, there was

DON'T FORGET OUR THEORY OF CHANGE

an element of representation for Indians in government, which increased all the way up to 1947.

Independence was won after a series of outcomes was achieved. It was not one continuous war which was finally decided on 15 August 1947. Think of it more like a series of battles and skirmishes in which one side (the INC) made slow but steady progress that led to the inevitable: the goal of independence being achieved.

An example of an actual Theory of Change is given at the end of this chapter. In brief it lays out the following:

1. What is the problem?
2. What is the impact of the problem?
3. What will the activist do?
4. What will the activist achieve?

It is important that this sequence be written out, even if it appears evident. By writing something down, we make our exercise formal, concentrate our mind on it, bring more focus to our effort and remove in some way the emotion from our thinking process. By writing it down, we take more control of the process. Activist organizations approach this exercise in a controlled and methodical manner. But there is no reason for it not to be done by each of us as individuals also.

And within organizations, individuals can further break down what their contribution and role is by producing their own Theory of Change exercise. For instance, if the task they are charged with has a weakness, how can this be addressed? If you look at it from this perspective, the exercise can be applied to any part of our life. It is just that we are setting down the problem in a way that we do not do in our personal or work lives. But it is merely the application of a logical structure that will usually produce better results than getting into problem solving without analysing the nature of the problem and the paths to a solution.

It is said about change that it always disappoints in the short term but surprises in the long term. This, in fact, is a reflection of the human attention span. We expect change to be visually evident, residing in spectacular moments. But the ways in which the circumstances for change are produced are often unspectacular, even though effective.

One way of looking at this is through what goes on in the technology industry. Insiders and even consumers are often unimpressed with changes in the current year's mobile phones. They appear to be the same as, or only marginally different from, the ones we used last year or the year before. But seen over a period of, say, fifteen years, the phones are so advanced and different that they might well be a different device altogether. But because the accumulated changes have come in a small and gradual manner, the user becomes desensitized to the dramatic shift.

Theory of Change explains the process of change by showing the causal linkages and the logic of the outcomes pathway. This means why one outcome is thought to be necessary to be achieved before the next one is. Structuring the problem and solution within the outcomes framework gives us precise links, helps us plan our efforts better and makes for better evaluation. In fact, it is the only way in which evaluation can be objectively done. How far one is along in achieving success can only be plotted on an identified pathway with marked signposts.

This is a comprehensive description and illustration of how and why a desired change is expected to happen. The key word here is 'expected to happen' and the exercise is focused on mapping out or filling in the missing middle. This means tracing what a programme or initiative for change does and how it leads to the desired goal being achieved.

Power Mapping Analysis

Once the problem and its impact are established, the next step is to identify who can deliver the change. The change here is to mitigate the impact and make it less severe over time till it is eliminated.

The principal agent of change could be the courts, the government, or the legislature. On a different scale, it could be a municipal official overseeing the road repair near your house, a school teacher, a postmaster or a neighbourhood doctor. It could even be a family member.

The change only happens when the institutions or individuals who have power over the change can be shifted from their current position to the one we want them to be in. This is understood through something called a Power Mapping Analysis. This is one of the most fun and interesting parts of the Theory of Change, because it lays out in clear and precise terms who holds power and how inclined they are towards taking our side.

A Power Analysis maps the holders of power along two axes. The vertical axis plots them in terms of how powerful they are, with the most powerful in terms of our objective being on top and the least powerful at the bottom. The horizontal axis plots them in terms of how much they oppose or support our objective (whether it is our goal or an outcome), from left to right. Strong opposition on the left and strong support on the right.

If an institution is powerful and opposed to what we seek, then it occupies the top left quadrant. If someone is powerful but neutral or uninterested in our objective, they will sit on the top of the centre line. If someone somewhat supports our objective and is not particularly powerful in terms of the change we want, they will be placed in the middle of the bottom right quadrant.

Power Mapping at an organizational level

When I was at Amnesty India, the organization joined a campaign to prevent the use of the potentially lethal pellet guns in Kashmir. And even though securing any change in the human rights condition of Kashmir was (and remains) difficult, we felt this was something we should throw ourselves at because it was achievable. And so we prepared Power Analysis Map to reach our goal: getting the State to stop using the weapon on protesters.

Here's what the map looked like:

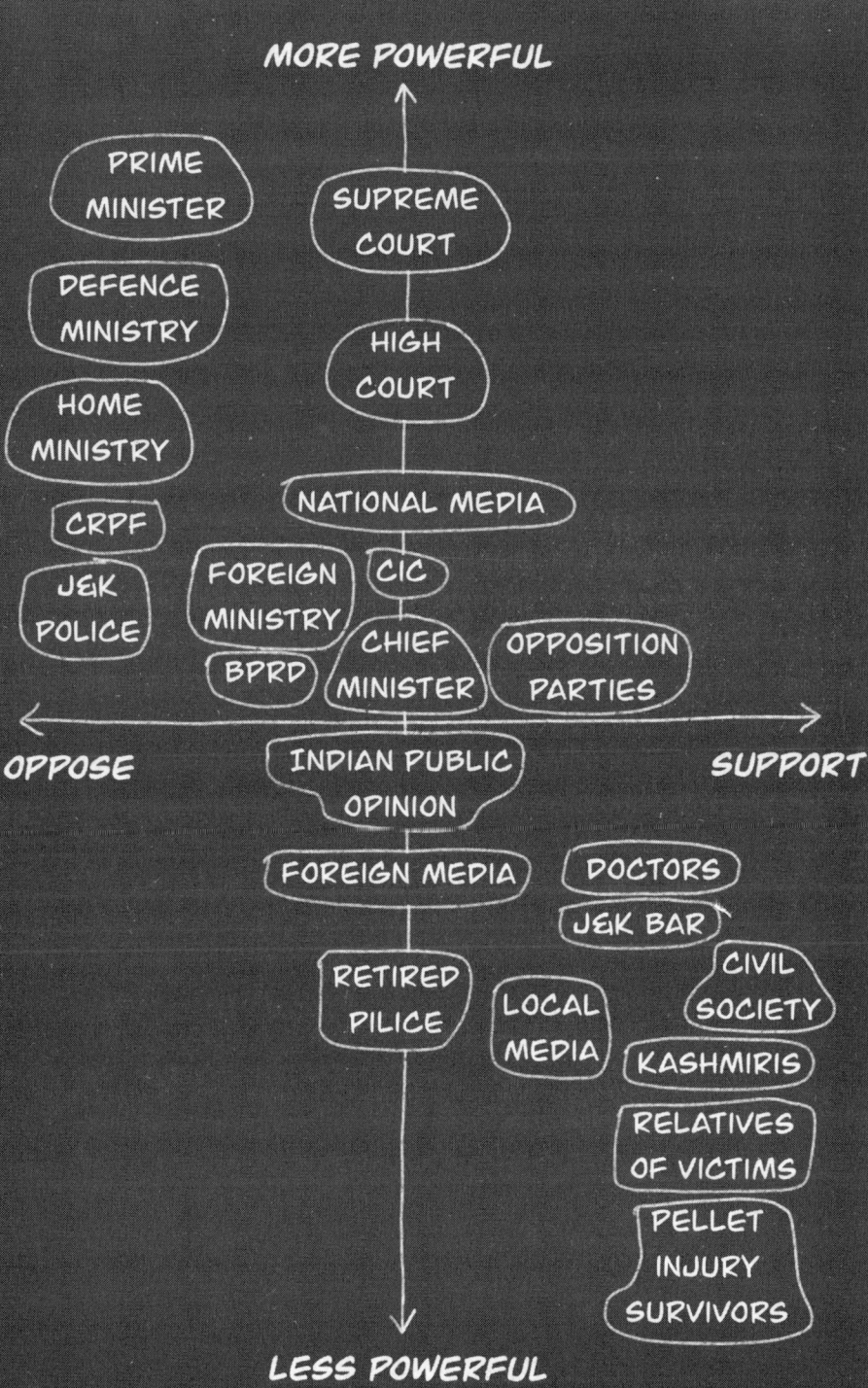

Let's examine why the individuals and institutions have been placed in the way they have.

It is strange to view the citizens of a democracy as weak, but this, generally, is the case in India and, especially, in Kashmir. Kashmiris do not want their government to use pellet guns against them but they cannot stop it. It is realistic therefore to place them in the way we have.

The chief minister would like to take the side of her citizens but cannot because she has no real power and is in many areas merely a figurehead.

The media in Kashmir is hamstrung in ways media elsewhere is not. It is reliant on government advertising for sustenance, is vulnerable to cases of sedition and other forms of harassment and preaches to the converted in terms of its readership. In the rest of India what the Kashmiri journalist says is looked on upon as 'anti-national'.

Pellet guns were being used against Kashmiris by both the Central government (the Ministry of Home Affairs in Delhi controls the Central Reserve Police Force in Kashmir) and by the J&K Police, controlled by the state government but only notionally. They have no interest in stopping their use of the weapon.

Doctors can provide evidence of the gun's destructive power on the human body but need a medium to transmit the message. The national media, with a few exceptions, was negatively disposed towards protesters.

The judiciary had the power to step in and stop the use of pellet guns on one of several grounds.

The first step on the road to justice was to establish the fact that the use of the pellet guns was unwarranted, unsafe and unjust. To do this, Amnesty India documented how the guns had blinded over one thousand Kashmiris, killed several of them (proving that its use did not meet the provision of reasonable force) and even hurt the security forces wielding them, because the projectiles it fired were uncontrollable.

The evidence was gathered through data collected from hospitals and through the Right to Information, interviews with survivors and surgeons, and through secondary sources like media reports. Without the credibility of this research, it would not have been possible to campaign on it.

The starting point for any movement for justice or change had to be the establishing of the facts. On the issue of the pellet guns, there was no dispute on the numbers. The government did not deny the harm the weapon causes: It insisted on using it nonetheless. And it would use it only against Kashmiris.[67]

One of the most important things the campaign did was attracting the attention of the world. India, quite rightly, does not want other countries interfering in what it sees as its internal affairs. But India is also a part of the global community, a signatory to covenants and declarations on human rights, and aspires to increase its membership status in several global bodies. For these reasons it must also concede to listen to these bodies. Which quadrant do you think the Office of the United Nations High Commissioner for Human Rights (OHCHR) would fall in our Power Analysis? Since the body is powerful and also inclined towards supporting the cause, it would be located in the top right.

OHCHR released two reports on Kashmir, in 2018 and in 2019.[68] There are more than fifty references to the weapon in the first report and twenty in the second.

The 2019 report reads: 'Indian security forces continue to use pellet-firing shotguns in the Kashmir Valley as a crowd-control weapon despite concerns as to excessive use of force and the large number of incidental civilian deaths and injuries that have resulted. It should be noted that this weapon is not deployed elsewhere in India. As noted in OHCHR's June 2018 report, the 12-gauge pump-action shotgun firing metal pellets is one of the most dangerous weapons used in Kashmir.'[69]

The US House of Representatives (which they call the Congress) had a resolution circulated in late 2019 which said that 'human rights observers have documented the police's use of excessive force against detained people and excessive and indiscriminate use of pellet shotguns, tear gas, and rubber bullets against protesters.'[70]

India managed to stave off a vote on this with difficulty and its foreign minister ducked a meeting at which the individual who tabled this resolution, Pramila Jayapal, was going to be present.

Four consecutive chief justices, T.S. Thakur, J.S. Khehar, Arun Misra and Ranjan Gogoi, heard the matter, which showed how important the issue had become. It was not possible for the government to use the weapon with impunity. And it was certainly not possible for it to use it freely without resistance—even if this was not strong resistance, much less a veto—from the judiciary and civil society.

As early as 2016, the Supreme Court said the government should 'apply its mind' before using the weapon and asked for an assurance that it wouldn't be used 'indiscriminately' and 'excessively'.[71]

In 2017, it asked the government to consider alternative and non-lethal methods of crowd control in place of the shotguns.[72]

In July 2019, the Supreme Court asked the Jammu and Kashmir High Court to decide 'in six weeks' a plea seeking to ban the use of the gun.[73]

As expected, the court did not ban the weapon; the judges said they were 'not inclined to prohibit the use of pellet guns in rare and extreme situations'.[74]

This ratcheted up some more pressure.

It all adds up in the end, and action, especially that which is thought through and concentrated at the right points of pressure, chips away at the problem.

Power Mapping at a local level

Now let us consider a Power Analysis concerning an individual who has a problem with garbage disposal in her neighbourhood. The garbage is not picked up regularly and the place is almost always dirty.

Who can she list as the individuals and groups to be influenced to effect change? The change being sought is clear: The garbage must be cleared regularly. The change agent is also clear: the local government body that is in charge of picking the garbage up.

The individual has several paths to approaching the problem. She could, of course, directly telephone or show up at the government office to see if the issue can be resolved. She must consider that the problem exists for a reason and that reason, whatever it may be, will need sufficient resistance to be opposed and overcome. Else, the problem will remain.

To solve it, information about what the root problem is may be necessary.

The Power Analysis here could be quite wide, and include political figures as well. But an effective path can also be charted through organizing and activating the residents' welfare association. Mobilizing the neighbourhood through a meeting where the issue is discussed and people are heard is an excellent way to go about this. Once there is an agreement that the problem exists and must be addressed, the momentum towards solving it builds up.

Even within this fairly limited framework, we can observe that another Power Analysis can be made on the neighbourhood or the housing society and which of the residents must the individual approach to make sure the issue is taken up with enthusiasm.

We have looked at where the points of change may reside in our Power Analysis. In the next chapter, let us consider what methods we can use to amplify or maximize our effort.

8

The Key Ingredients

This is a cookbook because it gives you the ingredients and the recipe to bake your own campaign for change—a series of options to choose from, depending on the objectives you want achieved.

These ingredients are tools used by activists and organizations globally. They are universal and have been proven to be effective for more than a century. They are the essential building blocks of civic change.

They may seem familiar and prosaic at first. But in reality, they are so powerful as to be almost magic. And they have become better with time.

Today, you and I have access to enormous reach in terms of communication and connectivity—unlike campaigners in the past—which is capable of producing and influencing change on a global scale.

Understanding the core ingredients, when to use them, what to mix them with and how effective they are likely to be is special knowledge, but not esoteric. In fact, all campaigning organizations use these ingredients in different ways and by different names. But they are the same.

Activist organizations respect the processes and tools—'ingredients'—which they use to try and bring about change. This is important to ensure that the quality and consistency of the recipe is maintained and that it can be prepared over and over again.

How can we, as individuals intending to become activists and campaigners, use them? Well, first we need to know and understand what they are. British writer C.S. Lewis opens *A Preface to Paradise Lost* with an instruction for all of us: 'The first qualification for judging any piece of workmanship from a corkscrew to a cathedral is to know what it is—what it was intended to do and how it is meant to be used. After that has been discovered, the temperance reformer may decide that the corkscrew was made for a bad purpose, and the communist may think the same about the cathedral. But such questions come later. The first thing is to understand the object before you: as long as you think the corkscrew was meant for opening tins or the cathedral for entertaining tourists, you can say nothing to the purpose about them.'

With this at the back of our minds, let us look at the tools of campaigning.

Research

Evidence-based campaigning organizations carry out research on the ground and then seek a change in laws or policies through a 'campaign', a fancy word for an organized course of action.

Once the evidence is established, the non-profit publishes it and seeks to open a debate on the issue. If a law is ineffective or harmful, it needs to go. For this to happen, the non-profit—and its campaigners, members and supporters—need to win the debate.

How does that happen? Only when the evidence is accepted by the authority that makes the law, the government, and it acts to make the change. This change is what is referred to as an outcome, which we've tackled in the last chapter. It is the desired goal produced by the activist's actions.

When the debate is not easily won (which is most of the time), other ingredients are used to bring about the change required. In most cases, laws or policies exist because they have existed for some time and there is not enough invested on the side of change. The inertia outweighs any momentum there might be for change. For the activist to bring the change about, she must bring the other ingredients into play to amplify what the research says.

Advocacy

What are some actions you can take to effectively promote your cause and influence decision makers?

Raising awareness: Ensuring that everyone knows about the issue, and from the organization's perspective, is the key objective here. In the old days (meaning twenty years ago), it meant hoping that the mainstream press would report on the research. This would make it better known by the citizenry and someone in politics might then pick it up. These days, social media is also a part of the media plan to make people more aware. We can reduce the message to a slogan and ensure that it is understood around the world (more on that in chapter 4).

Consumer pressure: You and I can influence the companies producing the products and services which want our business. This can encourage them, for instance, to source and produce more ethically. It can also get them to advertise ethically.

Following the attacks on Bollywood figures and general nastiness, the automaker Bajaj said in October 2020 that it would stop advertising with toxic news channels.[75] In May the same year, the website OpIndia lost revenue after a campaign by Stop Funding Hate forced advertisers like MUBI, Kiddylicious and LiveWorx off the platform.[76] This is how it happened: Stop Funding Hate tweeted an article in which OpIndia justified the boycott of Muslims. It then showed people how they could amplify the message. Their tweet read:

> Can you help alert more brands whose ads are on this toxic OpIndia article?
>
> 1. Go to the article: https://bit.ly/35cY9Dr
> 2. Take a screenshot showing the advertiser
> 3. Politely tweet the advertiser urging them to add OpIndia to their exclusion list cc-ing @StopFundingHate

This did three things in a single tweet. One, it showed the problem; two, it showed what the activist could do; and three, it guided them on how they could do it and what their targeted organization should do. Simple, direct and therefore effective.

Corporate pressure: Companies care about their image and are vulnerable to shareholder activism. Such pressure can come from individuals or groups.

Climate Action 100+, an investor initiative launched in 2017, pushes the most polluting companies to take action on climate change. This is a large body with over five hundred investors with a total of $47 trillion in assets (about fifteen times India's total Gross Domestic Product)—meaning that they can mount a lot of pressure on 100 'systemically important emitters,' accounting for two-thirds of annual global industrial emissions.

Political pressure: This is lobbying. It means to plead for support. Whose support? Those who have the direct or indirect power to bring about change. The targets are formal institutions, the State, political parties and international bodies. The Lok Sabha is literally the House of the people. It is our House. The MPs are representatives of the population, not their leaders. It is our right to approach them and inform them of what we think they should be doing and not doing. Yet, direct contact with elected representatives is not something Indians do as much as many other democracies. The contact with the State is primarily with the bureaucracy. But this is not because representatives choose to remain secluded: most of them keep open house in India. Walking over to their office or even home with an issue is not discouraged (try it). Because such activity is usually done by those who have a personal problem, such as a child's admission or an electricity connection, the person approached will likely remember you and your request. The larger the group approaching an elected representative, the more likely the person is to give a fair hearing and a promise of action.

In Amnesty folklore, a policy change was once brought about because the group approached an African president's mother and won her over to their side, thus getting the president to make a change on an issue he may not have been interested in before.

Remember that in a democracy, the Opposition, too, has power and influence. So it makes sense to approach elected representatives who may not currently be holding office.

> **FIND YOUR REPRESENTATIVE**
> http://loksabhaph.nic.in/Members/AlphabeticalList.aspx
> http://www.kla.kar.nic.in/assembly/member/mem_email.pdf
> https://bpac.in/b-engaged/know-your-corporator/

Crowdsourcing: Here you have a potent tool: social media. It gives you the power to rally large numbers of people to take action in support of your cause. It is the building of online communities that can exchange information and news, can raise money and can make known how wide a base of support your cause enjoys.

Mobilization

This is the hardest ingredient to get right. It is also the most effective one. It means organizing groups (hopefully very, very large groups) of people to take collective action. Mobilization can be done in different ways.

One is the circulation and signing of petitions, which is a frequent way in which change happens in some democracies. If enough people show interest in something, politics will naturally be attracted to it.

Then there is 'offline' or physical mobilization. This is less easy but usually more effective. It requires that people gather and take action: either hold a protest march or a sit-in (an Indian tactic known as a 'dharna').

The most successful mobilizers of recent times have been farmers' groups in Punjab and the women of Delhi's Shaheen Bagh. Such things bring the activists and their demand to the notice of those in power and begin the process of change.

LEVELS OF ENGAGEMENT

Activism takes many forms, and how people choose to engage or get involved with the cause can vary.

Organizing: This is leadership (but activists are modest, so they just call themselves organizers, not vice-president or general secretary).

It means bringing people together for a common cause. It could be getting the garbage cleared outside your house or ensuring your child's class gets less homework. It requires being able to coordinate and bringا concentration of force that will precipitate change.

Volunteering: This is participation and is one of the most fun parts of being an activist. There are few things as wonderful in life as being part of a community of like-minded people coming together for a cause they believe in passionately. Volunteering (we've got some tips later in this section on how you can participate) is also easy and the simplest path to beginning your journey as an activist. It offers you a range of experiences and can also be the route to discovering and building your skills.

Donating: Many activist organizations are funded by their own members, who see their donation as a kind of investment. Some have monthly membership fees and others a one-off payment (some organizations like Amnesty do not insist on money, but may require the prospective member to take action or participate).

Behaviour change: Ethical actions we take can influence those around us, especially those close to us. For example, turning vegan in support of animal rights is a powerful statement that an activist can make. Such actions do not only communicate personal belief and commitment but can also alter the way the world functions. In this instance, by making available vegan choice in restaurants and on airlines, making it easier for others to consider veganism.

Non-violent direct action

This is the hard end of activism. It requires confrontation with authority. Greenpeace often initiates non-violent direct action; for instance, by stopping a whaling ship from sailing. Gandhi's march to Dandi and the act of producing his own salt was a non-violent direct action, because it sought to disrupt the salt monopoly. Martin Luther King Jr. and other American activists who resisted segregation (the forcible separation of races on buses and in other public spaces) took non-violent direct action by occupying seats 'reserved' for white people.

In India, political parties, farmers' groups and other large organized forces regularly effect non-violent direct action. The bandhs, hartals, chakka jams and the creation of traffic and rail obstacles are all examples which are common to India. They are not, however, common to individual activists or small groups because there is the threat of getting into trouble with the authority. Some of us are willing to engage in direct action even if it means that there might be a fallout. The great American civil rights activist John Lewis welcomed it as 'good trouble, necessary trouble'. In his 2017 memoir, *Across That Bridge: A Vision for Change and the Future of America*, Lewis wrote: 'Freedom is not a state; it is an act. It is not some enchanted garden perched high on a distant plateau where we can finally sit down and rest. Freedom is the continuous action we all must take, and each generation must do its part to create an even more fair, more just society.'

Such lofty goals are achieved with the same steps and methods as the smaller ones that you and I seek to bring about.

Getting a campaign off the ground

All of the facets mentioned above, or some of them together, form what is called a campaign. It comes from a French word meaning the open countryside where battles are fought. A campaign seeks to make the most efficient possible use of all the forces available to produce victory. Some issues may need only research and media. Sometimes, research may not be required because the evidence is already at hand and visible to all. For example, climate change. Here, a campaign may be focused less on research and more on advocacy and mobilization.

In 2016, an activist group named Rising Up protested against the extension of Heathrow airport, which would increase pollution.

Their intention was to disrupt the airport's services, draw media attention, increase their membership and activist base by getting publicity, and put forward their side of the argument in the national debate.

The action involved fifteen individuals who chained themselves together and occupied the road leading up to the airport terminals. While the disruption was minimal (the State is very organized in ensuring that places such as airports function), the protesters received media coverage and made people aware of their cause.

In a document produced after the action ('Rising Up: Guide for Non-violent Direct Action'), the group shared its reflections and learnings. Its logistics team examined these questions to assess effectiveness.

The 'Rising Up' document assessed:

1. How to ensure disruption to the operations of the infrastructure targeted?
2. How to design actions which provoke arrests?
3. How to ensure the safety of all involved in the action, including when being removed from the scene by authorities?
4. How practical is the transportation and construction of the equipment used in the action?
5. What is the cost involved?

Once again, it is important to stress that they were operating in an environment where the State is tolerant. ('Do not try this at home!') They observed that the police did not want to arrest those individuals who attempted but could not effect road blockades. The police also did not arrest those that had engaged in the action but could be pulled out. This was also counterproductive because the activists sought to be arrested.

But it is different from the way in which police operate in India, especially with smaller groups.

Rising Up used bicycle locks, the kind that have u-shaped rods. One activist fastened it around their neck through the lock of another activist, binding them and making it difficult to move. They also devised a metal tube through which they put their arms from either side before fastening it.

The group's leaders had set themselves a target of attracting 100 volunteers to participate in the action. They got forty people to commit. Of these, thirty eventually arrived at Heathrow. Finally, fifteen were actually arrested in three separate groups.

Naturally, Rising Up concluded that it would have been more effective had it rehearsed. The group also had some basic lessons and how-tos. For instance:

- Making sure the workshop was included in their email send-out.
- Creating a Facebook event with the Rising Up account. Sharing it with friends and getting everyone in the Rising Up network to share it widely.
- Making individual phone calls and emails to individuals the group had met or had been put in touch with by the Outreach Working Group.

The objective they set out for—'disruption'—is, of course, viewed more benignly in their part of the world than it is in ours. In India, disruption is only allowed if the force disrupting is significant and the State is wary of it, such as political parties, which get away with disruption all the time. Individuals and civil society organizations have to be more modest in their approach, more careful and more aware of their own safety before they pick such a tactic.

Find Your Cause and Act				
My ingredients for change	Sign me up for	Random act of kindness	Biz of my dreams	Who am I?
Taking public transport, walking or riding a bike instead of driving—and encouraging others to do the same.	A bike-riding campaign that encourages people to use pedal power instead of cars.	Picking up litter.	Organizing climate strikes for students across your school district.	Climate Change-Maker, interested in stopping global warming.
Feeding birds by hanging a simple feeder in your balcony or attaching one to a window.	Making a nature or wildlife documentary like Blue Planet.	Looking after a neighbour's pet while they're away.	Making homemade bath and body products using natural ingredients and no animal products.	Animal Advocate, who believes animals deserve as much kindness and respect as humans.

My ingredients for change	Sign me up for	Random act of kindness	Biz of my dreams	Who am I?
Saving paper and cutting down on waste by printing only when necessary and on both sides. Writing on old envelopes and send e-cards instead.	Setting up a battery recycling station for your school.	Writing a 'get well soon' card on recycled paper.	A 'green' gift-wrapping service using recycled paper or newspaper.	Zero-Waste Hero, making better use of what I already have.
Buying a reusable water bottle.	Turning milk cartons into bird feeders for the school playground.	Donating old books or toys to public schools or charities.	Starting a beach clean-up club, organizing groups of people to pick up litter on the beach.	Anti-plastic Pioneer interested in helping stop plastic pollution.

9

The Hidden Hazards

Before we begin, we must examine the elephant in our room. Activism often has consequences for the activist. These can range from being alienated by friends and family (who may not necessarily know or understand why you have chosen to become 'political') and facing abuse on social media to, in some cases, legal trouble.

Let me tell you about my own experiences.

On 11 June 2020, I got an email from Twitter saying my account had been 'withheld' because of a legal notice from the government. The offence? I retweeted a 31 May video from the Colorado Times Recorder. The original tweet described the video in these words: 'Incredible scene at Colorado's Capitol right now. Thousands of protesters are lying face down with their hands behind their backs chanting "I can't breathe." They're doing this for nine mins. #copolitics #denverprotest #GeorgeFloyd.'

My retweet carried this text: 'We need protests like these. From Dalits and Muslims and Adivasis. And the poor. And women. World will notice. Protest is a craft.'

My neighbourhood police inspector registered a case accusing me of inciting violence. The case was filed suo motu, which in India's quaint legalese means the State itself was the complainant. Of all the police stations in India, it was my neighbourhood one that took offence. Asked by the BBC why the case had been filed, Bengaluru's police commissioner said my tweet was dangerous because it instigated people to gather at a time when Covid-19 protocols were in place.[77]

I wrote to Twitter asking for a copy of the legal order from the government so I could challenge it in court, but they did not reply. After online protests in my support (activists stand up for each other all the time), Twitter reinstated my account, partially at first—making it fully accessible to those outside India but preventing those in the country from accessing my homepage—and, a few days later, completely. Three weeks later, on 2 July, a BJP legislator in Surat filed another case against me, this time under a non-bailable offence, for a tweet recording the official history of the community Modi is from[78].

The thing is that someone else might have tweeted the same things and not got into trouble. It was not the content of the tweets that was problematic for the State; it was, to a large extent, the person.

Activists, once identified, tend to be targeted for what they stand for. This is something you should know. I do what I do because I cannot do otherwise and cannot look away. But I also understand that there will be others who choose to have a lower profile about such things or try and keep their activism anonymous.

With that in mind, let us move on.

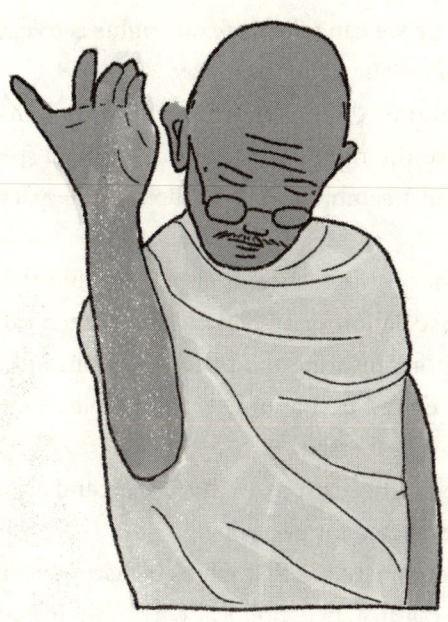

Are Indians really free to protest and to take individual actions?

We can broadly divide the world into two kinds of nations. Those where individuals have their rights guaranteed legally and where the State upholds them for the most part: North America, African nations such as South Africa, and large parts of Europe. Other nations, such as China and North Korea, restrict civil liberties and democratic rights by law.

India is different from both sets. We have fundamental rights and civil liberties guaranteed by our Constitution, but the State is reluctant to let us enjoy them.

The pretense of the rights being available is maintained, but, in large part, the rights are denied. We have examined in detail how our fundamental rights are encroached upon by the State in Section I of this book (p. 14).

The only way we can take back our rights is to claim them.

India is also unique in another way.

In some nations, there is more freedom than in others to act. Individuals have the right to association and free speech, but their right to peaceful assembly also gives them more space than in other nations.

In some other nations, there is either very limited or no right to free speech, association or assembly. Free speech can be restricted by controlling or censoring the press. Freedom of association can be limited or ended by banning political parties or groups and forbidding the membership.

In India, the rights exist as we have seen and are restricted. But they are not restricted for everyone.

Direct action, including that which is disruptive, is 'allowed' for some groups. For instance, political parties themselves call bandhs which are coercive and often even violent. Organized groups like farmers' groups, caste-based groups and trade unions can engage in direct action that is disruptive, but, in some sense, allowed or at least tolerated. They can stop the functioning of the railways, block highways and carry out marches involving hundreds of thousands of people to bring to a halt activity in city centres.

The State does not have the appetite to engage with these large and organized groups and looks away when they do the same thing that others can be arrested for or prevented from doing.

The rule of law is flexible in these instances and not applied as firmly as it would be in other places.

Even the Supreme Court wants protests by Indians to be carried out in so-called designated areas. This is to ensure that the protesters do not disturb the activity of others, including the State. This also ensures, though this is a byproduct, that the protesters are not heard. There are protests that have carried on continuously for years in designated areas like Jantar Mantar in central Delhi, with no result.

The physical threat of protest

At the beginning of this chapter, I've shared how participation in protest can have personal consequences. Taking part in it can also pose a potential physical threat too.

Sometimes, violence takes place at protests. It may be perpetuated by protesters or non-protesters (i.e., outsiders) who take advantage of the simmering resentment. Then, there are times when the authorities clamp down on peaceful protests. These crackdowns have the potential to ignite counter-violence by protesters.

Earlier in the book, I've talked about a special crowd-control weapon used in only one place in the world, Kashmir. The pellet gun can more accurately be described as a 12-gauge shotgun that fires birdshot. This is the same gun used to shoot clay pigeons. The birdshot is in a cartridge that contains about five hundred lead balls.

Once shot, the cartridge explodes and the pellets disperse in all directions, harming everyone in their path. There is no way to control their trajectory or direction. Pellet shotguns, by their very nature, are inaccurate—and the effects of their use are indiscriminate.

In the eight months between July 2016 and February 2017, a total of 6,221 people suffered pellet gun injuries, including 782 eye injuries.[79] The actual figures relating to the devastation caused by these weapons are likely to be even higher.

At least fourteen people have died as a result of pellet injuries since 2010.[80] Amnesty India also obtained information through RTI applications which suggests that at least sixteen J&K Police personnel suffered pellet injuries in 2016.[81]

Due to their nature, pellet shotguns have been responsible for blinding, killing and traumatizing thousands of people in Kashmir. Amnesty's briefing sought to shed light on the immeasurable harm that people in Kashmir have suffered because of the use of these shotguns. Besides the serious physical injuries, many show symptoms of psychological trauma and all of them face everyday struggles: dealing with the darkness that has descended on their lives, having to let go of simple pleasures, preparing for difficult futures.[82]

How to protect yourself during a protest

Activism sometimes comes with risks. So being prepared is the best way to stay safe. These are some pointers to keep in mind:

1. Security concerns vary from person to person. While some advocacy organizations encourage people to put everything on the line, many activists are risk averse. A diverse group of people who come together for a cause can only build a strong rapport if they agree to care for one another. The first step is to talk about security measures openly with the team.
2. Make a list of the threats you may face and create a clear plan of action with your fellow protesters.
3. Identify who you are protecting yourselves from and whom you can collaborate with to stay safe.
4. Identify potentially harmful events and review any possible changes in the security situation at routine team meetings.
5. Make sure you know what your rights are. While Section I of this book covers your fundamental rights, Section IV of this book sheds light on legislation that may affect you.

AN IDEAL GIRL

Gets up in the morning

Applies consumer pressure

Pushes corporates

Exerts political pressure

Spreads awareness

Organizes community

Volunteers at NGOs

Mobilizes online

Donates what she can

Changes own behaviour

Takes direct action

Brushes teeth at night

10

Make It to MasterChef Level

You may have come across this quotation before: 'Never doubt that a small group of thoughtful, committed citizens can change the world; indeed, it is the only thing that ever has.'

The keyword here, and this might be surprising to some, is not committed. Of course, commitment is required, but it is also assumed among activists that they will be committed. If they weren't interested in change, they wouldn't be activists.

The keyword is thoughtful. It is the thoughtful ones among them that are more likely to deliver change. What does thoughtful mean?

It means that campaigning and activism is a science, a craft that has to be learned. It is not the passion of the activist that makes her effective so much as her ability to deploy that passion across her toolbox of ingredients and recipes.

If we look at activists across the generations, we notice that they often have individual strengths that are unique. For instance, Gandhi's innovative coinage of words like satyagraha for activism; Medha Patkar's focused dedication on one issue, the Narmada and dams on it; Rana Ayyub's courageous persistence in exposing majoritarianism. Amnesty International and Greenpeace were headed by an individual, Kumi Naidoo, who used music and singing as a means to galvanize gathered activists and was thus able to infuse energy into them. And though all of them are different in some ways, they are the same in one way: They are all thoughtful about how it is that they will go about their activism.

Activism without method, without contemplation of how to move through the programme towards a goal, will usually remain unfulfilled.

Long-term thinking is your best short-term strategy

Activism is not taught in our schools but it must be and should be. It is how we can influence change, perhaps the most important skill we can learn. In the context we are talking about here, activism is individual action with social consequences. This is the definition of activism by Duncan Green in his book *How Change Happens*.[83] Much of it involves collective activity.

Tim Gee, in his book *Counterpower: Making Change Happen*,[84] documents how countries won civil rights victories. The case studies include India's freedom struggle, the ending of the Vietnam war and Apartheid in South Africa. He says all protest movements in history have had the same internal debates.

Anxious activists have asked themselves:

- Do protests make a difference?
- How important is the sympathy of the mainstream media?
- Does breaking (or bending) the law hinder the cause?

This is quite true. The issues of making a difference plays on the minds of all activists. And they have always been told: 'But nothing will change.' The thing is that progress disappoints in the short run, but surprises in the long run. Think of the example of mobile phones cited earlier and how they improve year on year.

The markers and signals of progress are not always visible or apparent. Change is happening all the time. If we look at it in the widest frame, it is positive change.

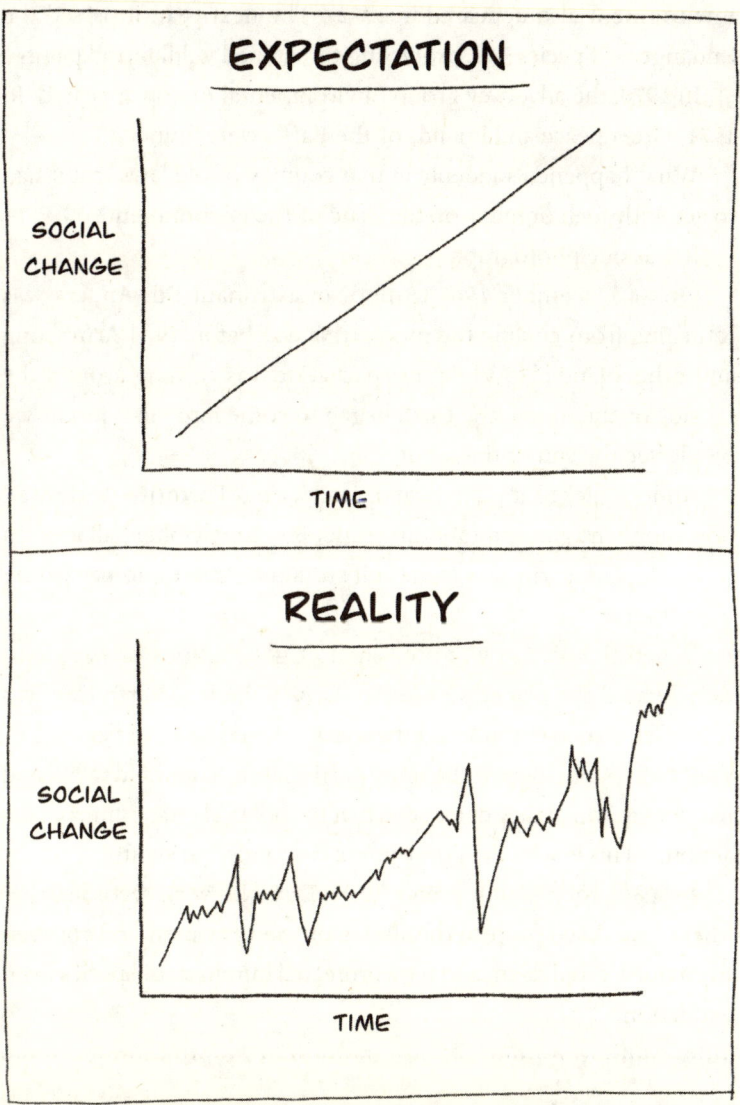

A PHOTO THAT SPARKED A MOVEMENT

In 1970, the US government formed the Environmental Protection Agency and tightened the Clean Air Act. In 1972, it passed the Clean Water Act, governing water pollution. The same year, it passed the Environment Pesticide Control Act (Britain's Department of the Environment also appeared in 1972). The next year, it passed the Endangered Species Act, protecting threatened wildlife and plants.

In 1970, the advocacy group Environmental Action appeared. In 1971, Greenpeace and Friends of the Earth were founded.

What happened suddenly in that country of old laws that it had to act with such urgency on the issue of the environment?

It was one photograph.

On 24 December 1968, American astronaut Bill Anders was returning from circling the moon (this was before Neil Armstrong and others landed). While his spacecraft was coming around the far side of the moon, the earth began to come into view, just as we would see the sun or the moon rise.

Anders clicked a photograph, later called Earthrise. It showed how alone, fragile and rare our planet is, a lonely blue ball in a sea of black. The earth was like a self-sustaining spaceship navigating the universe.

When this image was published, it got millions of people to rally behind the planet. On 22 April 1970, the first Earth Day was celebrated, an event in which two crore Americans (10 per cent of their total population of the time) participated. They held rallies and marches in which they demanded that the political establishment take action.[85] This is why the government responded so swiftly.

In its history of the event, Earth Day Network recorded that 'these laws have protected millions of men, women and children from disease and death and have protected hundreds of species from extinction.'

The power of social media activism

Social media is your hidden superpower. It may appear mundane, given its prevalence and its use. But it is a tool of staggering power. Let us see the ways in which it is special.

First, it is free. It doesn't cost anything to open an account. And all accounts start off the same. There is no difference between one Instagram account and another and it is up to the user to try and build on what they have. Of course, there are some natural advantages that some have (such as celebrities with large followings). This, however, does not mean that the rest of us are in any way disadvantaged from making use of the medium.

Second, social media helps you take action and helps you let others take action. Liking something, retweeting it and replying to it is a means of engaging with a subject. When we offer support to a community that is under attack by taking up its cause, we attract others towards us who are like-minded. Floating a poll or a petition is easy and lets others notice us.

Third, you can extend this a step further and mobilize. This is just another term for gathering together people who share concerns. Social media is terrific for forming groups and subgroups of people. It also is a tool for getting people together on the street and in meetings. People's Union for Civil Liberties has a WhatsApp group (of which I am a part) where we regularly share news and updates and plan our online and offline activities. Hashtags were invented and are used for this reason. In an instant, you can connect yourselves to large numbers of people invested in the same things that you are.

Fourth, social media allows you to reach the people that you want to without a filter. If your campaign plan requires you to directly communicate with a part of the government (to put forward a concern you have) or with a celebrity (to amplify your message), you have the ability to do so. And as you become more connected with your solidarity groups online, it becomes easier for you to reach out to such people because others will join you. I know plenty of people on Twitter who are otherwise unknown but have managed to develop a formidable presence, purely because of the interests they hold and the amount of energy they put in to ensure they are heard.

Fifth, social media is always on. This is obvious and sounds like a basic thing. However, it removes one obstacle of activism. Often, things may be planned or desired, but may not get carried out. Let's say, a campaign to write letters to some authority over a polluting plant. This is how activism used to happen a few decades ago. It required physical effort to ensure that letters were written, gathered, posted to the right addresses and then followed-up on. With social media, this has all been folded into one step. If you have an idea, you can execute it instantly.

Sixth, global reach. Campaigns often have a component that needs engagement with groups or entities abroad. For instance, a climate change campaign often concerns multiple nations and organizations. Social media gives us the mechanism to not only reach all those entities directly but also lets us build global solidarity groups. And it allows us to join such groups that already exist.

Seventh, it is easy. There is nothing that prevents us from posting messages, photographs and videos on our accounts. Some can do it better than others, but all can improve through practice and observation of what others are doing. This is one of the things that has made social media the phenomenon it is in our time: It gives easy access to all those who want to participate.

Eighth, it does away with the reliance on traditional media. Previously, groups had to be dependent on newspapers and television to take their message to the people. And this control is often exercised tightly in nations such as India by the media. They act as a gatekeeper for content and will turn down stories they do not agree with. Many news outlets charge money for carrying material that is not reported directly by them. Social media liberates us from all of this and gives us agency.

Ninth, because of a lack of dependence on the traditional media, social media lets us have a 'dog in the fight'. Meaning that if there is an issue of importance that is being debated in the public realm, say attacks on churches or hate speech against Muslims, social media gives us the space to express our view which might not be the one the State or the media may want expressed. Again, this must be emphasized that not that long ago, the dissenting view often did not get any airtime or space. No longer.

Tenth, it allows us to raise our profile in the public realm. We are in activism and want others to know what it is that we stand for. Social media is today's equivalent of the soapbox in England a century ago. People would come to parks with a little box that gave them an elevated platform to hold forth. If the material interested passers-by, they would stop and listen. Your Twitter and Insta accounts are the same thing—except with global reach, lot more people available to talk to, and the ability to join in with those who feel similarly.

The pandemic has strengthened social media as the preferred and dominant medium that campaigning organizations use to reach out and mobilize. This was already a transition that was happening, but has now become solid and permanent.

What we have examined in the points above has already manifested itself on the groups that have been active in the pandemic. The Black Lives Matter protests used so successfully to mobilize voters were a great example of an online/offline campaign. This period has also helped end a myth about the supposed lack of effectiveness of social media activism (what we have noted is referred to as 'slacktivism'). It has shown that social media activity is as effective and legitimate as anything else. Indeed, we must reconsider using the word 'virtual' because what happens on social media is just as material and real as what happens elsewhere.

11

Put Your Hand Up

One of the quickest ways to become an activist is to become a member of an existing group working on rights issues in India. They all welcome participation from individuals and will be happy to have a chat with you about what they do and what you can do with them.

These groups are not rivals and do not compete against each other. They often work together on issues and many individuals are members of more than one of these.

People's Union for Civil Liberties (PUCL) was founded by Jayaprakash Narayan, who united the Opposition against the Emergency. PUCL's functions are to increase consciousness about human rights and civil liberties; to provide a platform for all groups, including political parties, to come together for furthering human rights; to creatively use institutions like the courts and the press so that they may become more sensitive to the human rights situation in India; and to intervene directly in cases where violations of human rights take place.

It is a membership organization and the fees begin at ₹10.

Website: http://www.pucl.org/get-involved
Twitter: @PUCLIndia

Human Rights Law Network (HRLN), founded in 1989, uses the legal system to advance human rights, fight violations and ensure access to justice for all. It provides free legal aid to individuals and works in twenty-four states.

HRLN welcomes lawyers, students, social activists, grassroots workers, economists, anthropologists, researchers, academics, political activists, artists, media and communications specialists, web and graphic designers, event planners, marketers, accounts specialists and project managers. It welcomes contributions, with no minimum amount.

Email: contact@hrln.org
Twitter: @HRLNIndia

Safai Karmachari Andolan is a movement for the elimination of manual scavenging (the practice of cleaning, carrying and disposing of human excrement from dry latrines or sewers). It is present nationally and holds rallies and events attended by thousands of people, including a diverse range of people from other civil society groups.

Website: https://www.safaikarmachariandolan.org/volunteer

Citizens for Justice and Peace (CJP) was relaunched in 2017. It is focused on the rights of minorities (religious, ethnic, caste, gender and sexual minorities as well as persons with disabilities), freedom of expression, reform of the criminal justice system and child rights. CJP welcomes contributions with no minimum amount.

Website: https://cjp.org.in/volunteer/
Twitter: @CJPIndia

Greenpeace India uses non-violent creative action for a greener planet. The fifty-year-old global body has long had a presence in India and is the most innovative protest group when it comes to direct action in public spaces.

Greenpeace has a WhatsApp Activism community, which interacts weekly. WhatsApp the word 'Hello' to +916366891347.

Greenpeace welcomes contributions with no minimum amount.

Website: https://www.greenpeace.org/india/en/

Amnesty India is part of the Nobel Peace prize winning Amnesty International movement. It has been present in some form or other in India since the late 1960s when former Union Minister George Fernandes was a member. It publishes reports on rights violations and then campaigns on them. Amnesty operates a global group that appeals for urgent action when a person is under threat of imminent and grave human rights abuse.

Amnesty organizes events and fundraisers and you can volunteer with it.

Website: https://amnesty.org.in/get-involved/volunteer-with-us/

The group invites memberships of ₹600 a month as well as contributions with no minimum amount.

 SAFAI KARMACHARI ANDOLAN

These are some of the groups that you can consider working with. There are many that work on different rights. Participation itself will help you understand the space and its people better.

How to volunteer

The civil society space is informal and friendly. Walking up to a protest site or an organization's office and asking what is going on and what you can volunteer for will usually be productive.

The many Shaheen Bagh-like groups formed across India were all run by volunteers, most of whom were participating in their first protest. Volunteers serve food, help with transportation, make posters, distribute pamphlets, make announcements, coordinate with speakers, write out applications and do any number of things that do not require training. Volunteering will give you access to new people (and especially new types of people) and to information and knowledge.

Volunteers can often get global opportunities. Many international civil society organizations use volunteers from across the world for their annual conferences and meetings.

Volunteers often take jobs in civil society and the organizations including the ones listed above employ researchers, fund raisers, advocates, administrators, accountants, managers, campaigners and many other types of people. Some of the civil society jobs currently available can be seen on this website:

http://www.devnetjobsindia.org

NGOs anticipate volunteers and have a path planned for their growth in the organization. This is called a Supporter Journey. It has stages of involvement and participation and there will be people in the organization that will take you through them. The stages are defined by your experience and begin at the starting point, where you have none. You do not have to do anything other than putting your hand up.

Someone once said that 90 per cent of success was just showing up. This is certainly true for volunteering.

How to start an affinity group

Affinity is a liking for something because of interest. An affinity group is five or more people who work together autonomously on direct actions or other projects. There is no leader in such groups. This absence of a hierarchical leadership is generally one of the defining things about civil society. An affinity group is opposed to top-down decision making, which is what leadership generally implies.

It is important people join an affinity group that is best suited to their interests. Think of it as a club or a fraternity. Participants should consider who would be willing to do the same sort of work they do and take the same sort of risks—be it exposing oneself to hate on social media, losing one's job because of an unpopular opinion, or, of course, getting into trouble with the State.

Affinity groups that have members with different skills are more likely to be effective. A mix of individuals—some with social media skills, some with research abilities and interests and some who can organize an outdoor event—will likely get more done.

Individuals who might be unwilling to go on a physical protest may be good at making posters that others can take with them. Given how diverse a set of skills is needed for campaigning in its many forms, there are lots of things where people can fit in because of some natural talent or propensity. Of course, the group will have to build trust. Many affinity groups are those that have existed for years (one such group is PUCL, which only has informal links between members but has been active and effective in its rights work for decades). Affinity groups are loose and fluid rather than with a fixed hierarchical and corporate-type structure. Individuals come and go and the group changes with time.

What can an affinity group do?
It can be used for all kinds of actions, whether mass or on a smaller scale. Affinity groups can be used to drop a banner, do street theatre, gather for a march, take out a rally, organize sit-ins, change the message on a large hoarding, play music and sing songs (music and singing is important to protests). They could just get people together at home over a cup of tea and samosas and discuss an issue in depth.

This open discussion and debate about something is key. Building a consensus (civil society groups around the world generally operate with greater degree of agreement and consensus than the private sector) is important. Consensus does not mean a decision everyone wants—rather, it's a decision everyone is willing to accept. Good discussions require a facilitator, a person that civil society is familiar with but perhaps does not exist in the corporate world or the workplace.

A facilitator ensures that meetings of the affinity group run smoothly and effectively. Their role is to ensure that the group achieves its objectives in the meeting. They do not make decisions for the group, but suggest ways to help it move forward and collectively reach decisions. A facilitator can also help ensure everyone is able to participate in the meeting and that it is not dominated by a few individuals. You can appoint one person to facilitate all the meetings, or rotate who takes on this role at each meeting. Rotating the responsibility is usual in most civil society groups. A facilitator has no administrative or managerial or decision-making power but her task is to be responsible for putting an event or an action together, or even just to ensure that a discussion takes place in orderly fashion with everyone being given a chance to give their input. Activists have the same traits of shyness and dominance like the rest of us. Respect for what everyone says and feels is critical in such groups.

Each group, however small, needs an agreement or a charter on how it will operate and how its decisions will be made. At some point, it will also need to agree on what it does, how it acts and how it will react in certain situations. This may not be easy to do at first. But having decision-making out in the open makes it easier and more acceptable. Doing this properly the first time ensures that an enormous amount of time is ultimately saved. It may help to break the group up into pairs that can look out for each other.

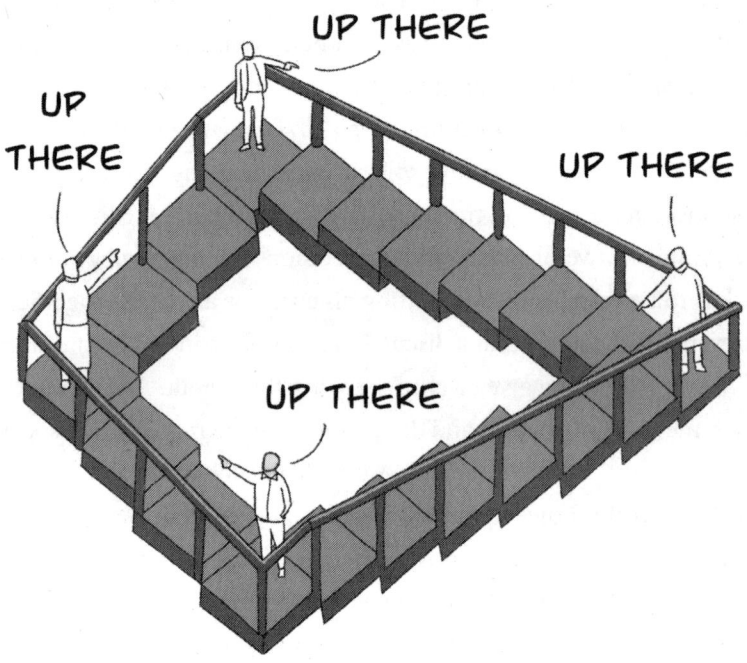

How to start a campaign

Campaigns are mostly about communications and involve a conversation.

Persuade people to act. Think of it exactly like an advertising campaign, which works in the same manner: Someone wants you to act in a way that you are not currently acting. The way is to get you to buy their product or service. Let's say it is a packet of biscuits.

The manufacturer wants you to act (make a purchase) but has no means of influencing you other than messaging (advertisement).

The Ambanis, Adanis, Tatas and Birlas do not need to campaign because they can achieve what they seek by influencing the State individually.

For NGOs, the only real resource to secure change is public persuasion.

Corporate campaigns don't have to appeal to anyone's better nature.

Scientists progress campaigns by research, writers by publishing. You and I by acting.

Campaigning gives you agency and greater direct influence over the world.

In his book, *How to Win Campaigns: Communications for Change*, Chris Rose says that campaigns:[86]

1. are wars of persuasion. They involve mostly communications.
2. involve conversations, especially with those you do not know.
3. persuade people to act.
4. are like advertising (though corporate campaigns don't appeal to people's better nature).
5. are the common politics of the people.

6. for NGOs, the only resource to secure change in public persuasion.
7. are done in different ways. Scientists progress campaigns by research, writers through publishing
    i. formal statements (speeches, signed statements, mass petitions, declarations)
    ii. communications (tweets, FB posts, banners, posters, letters to newspapers)
    iii. joint representation (rallies, gatherings)
    iv. symbolic actions (wearing symbols, destruction of own property, protest disrobings, displaying flags and portraits, renaming signs)
    v. pressure on officials (vigils, dharnas)
    vi. art (music, singing, street plays)
    vii. processions (marches, parades, motorcades)
    viii. withdrawal (walk-outs, silence, turning one's back)

SECTION III

Successful Protests of Our Time (and What You Can Learn from Them)

12

It Was One Tweet
(#MeToo, 2017)

One individual's act of resistance, it brought down a minister in the most powerful government India had seen in decades. And then she won a court victory against the man she had bravely taken on. The case was that of journalist Priya Ramani, who first wrote an article on 13 October 2017, naming an unidentified former boss of hers. She was twenty-three and he forty-three when he called her to his hotel room and made passes at her, inviting her to sleep with him.

On 8 October 2018, Ramani tweeted out the man's name: M.J. Akbar, a junior foreign minister in the Narendra Modi government. A week later, Akbar filed a defamation suit against Ramani.

By this time, however, several women had joined Ramani. The revelation and Akbar's aggressive response prompted as many as twenty women, also survivors of Akbar's predatory behaviour, to tell their stories.

This was a flashpoint in India's #MeToo movement. After all, it involved an allegation about an event that had occurred a quarter century ago. And yet it could not be waved away. Two days after filing the suit, Akbar was forced to resign in the face of intense media scrutiny.

A few days after this, *The Washington Post* published a column by the highly respected business editor of *NPR* (America's public radio station network) accusing Akbar of rape.[87] Akbar was suspended by the Editors Guild of India and the trial began soon after. Despite facing pressure, Ramani refused a settlement with Akbar and chose to fight the case instead.

Ramani was acquitted of defamation charges on 17 February 2021, with woman after woman taking the stand and testifying to being harassed in similar fashion. They were brave enough to go through their experience and put it in the public domain. The judge said, referring to Akbar's defence that he was a man of standing, that 'even a man of social status can be a sexual harasser'. And that 'sexual abuse takes away dignity and self-confidence, and that the right of reputation cannot be protected at the cost of right to dignity'.[88] On the time that had passed before Ramani accused Akbar—usually seen as something that is in favour of the accused—the judge rightly observed that a 'woman has right to put her grievance even after decades'.

The critical thing about this case is that it began with a single person and a single article. It was one tweet, one year after the article had been written, which led to the resignation, the court case and the acquittal. That should tell us the importance of individual action, however small, when it is brave.

Ramani's was the most striking Indian victory in the global #MeToo movement, which took off around 2016 and 2017. First, accusations by multiple women against the powerful chairman and CEO of Fox News, Roger Ailes, led to his resignation in July 2016, days after being accused. One of the top anchors of the channel, Bill O'Reilly, also lost his job the following year after he was accused and advertisers pulled out from his show.

The second and more famous episode that triggered #MeToo globally began with a report in *The New York Times*. It said that the powerful Hollywood producer Harvey Weinstein had been systematically sexually harassing and sexually assaulting women, including actors, for years. Weinstein had produced some of the biggest films in Hollywood. His circle of friends included the Clintons and Barack Obama.

His behaviour, however, was an open secret, whispered about in showbiz circles for decades. In 2015, an Italian model recorded Weinstein apologizing for groping her. The authorities did not feel this met the threshold of a crime and refused to charge Weinstein. This was in keeping with the time—remember this was as recently as 2015—when a man would usually get away with behaviour which is today seen as intolerable (all because of #MeToo). The 2017 report said Weinstein had, for years, been paying off women he had abused and who had confronted him. This and other reports on Weinstein encouraged several women to testify against him in court. Weinstein was convicted of sexual assault and jailed in 2020.

Each of these three men—Akbar, Ailes and Weinstein—were faced initially by the accusation of a single woman: Priya Ramani, Fox News anchor Gretchen Carlson and the Italian model Ambra Battilana. Once the expected exchange had happened—with the accused individual not only denying but attempting to slander the accuser—others joined in and took the predator down.

On 16 October 2017, actress Alyssa Milano tweeted: 'If you've been sexually harassed or assaulted, write "me too" as a reply to this tweet.' More than sixty thousand people responded.

Much of this solidarity helped take the fear and shame away from survivors and victims.

This format repeated itself several times over.

The actor Kevin Spacey was accused by a man of sexually harassing him when he was a minor. Spacey did not face trial but lost his projects, including his role in the hit series *House of Cards*.

There were others, too, who were accused of sexual harassment and lost their jobs. Roy Price, the head of Amazon Studios, who was initially accused in 2015 but could not survive the #MeToo movement in 2017. The same year, US gymnastics doctor Larry Nassar was accused and later sentenced to a long jail term for sexually abusing gymnasts who came to him for treatment. The Republican candidate for Alabama senator, Roy Moore, lost his election after women, some of them minors, accused him of harassment. He became the first person from his party to lose a statewide poll in a quarter century. Democratic Senator Al Franken resigned from his position in 2018 after women revealed being harassed by him. NBC news anchor Matt Lauer was fired, also in 2017, after women came forward to say he assaulted them.

Comedian Louis C.K., accused by five women of sexual misconduct, apologized and was dropped from various projects which he said cost him $35 million (about ₹250 crore). Celebrity chef

Mario Batali, Topshop billionaire Philip Green, CBS Chief Executive Les Moonves, Google Android creator Andy Rubin, singer R Kelly (who was convicted in 2021), tenor Placido Domingo, and comedian Bill Cosby (convicted and jailed for sexual assault in 2018 after years of allegations) were also among the famous individuals brought to justice by #MeToo. A *New York Times* report said 201 powerful men had lost their positions because of the #MeToo movement, and these were only the cases that were known to the media.[89]

Lessons we learned: #MeToo's greatest win was not the fact that many famous individuals paid the price for their actions. It was that that the individual making the accusations now was believed by the world, received the support that was denied to others in the past, and the accused was not able to brush off his actions.

It also led to systemic change. For instance, states in the US began to ban non-disclosure agreements that covered sexual harassment. Those who tolerated egregious behaviour in their organizations were told to go, including the founder of Uber, Travis Kalanick.

And, of course, its success included the fact that #MeToo was a global movement, receiving considerable support from the Arab world too.

13

The Strength of Unbroken Resistance
(NO CAA, NO NPR, NO NRC, 2020)

The single most inspiring protest globally for many in India and around the world was the one at Shaheen Bagh, a middle-class neighbourhood near the Jamia Millia Islamia university in Delhi.

After the Babri Masjid was demolished in 1992, Muslims left mixed neighbourhoods and began to become more ghettoized in urban areas like Shaheen Bagh for safety. Few outside the area knew of its existence till December 2019, when, in a matter of days, this little neighbourhood became famous around the world. It provided Indians a model for protest and resistance, a model that could be, and was, replicated easily and effectively and meaningfully.

Before we revisit its story, we need to understand the government's citizenship matrix that set it off.

In January 2018, a team from the National Human Rights Commission (NHRC) visited two detention camps in Assam, where those who could not prove their citizenship were being held. This was the final phase of the National Register of Citizens in that state, where those marked out by the government as being 'doubtful' for any reason had to prove their credentials. Those who could not, would end up in these detention centres.

The three-person team (Dr Mahesh Bhardwaj, Harsh Mander and Indrajeet Kumar) found a situation of grave and extensive human distress.[90] The detainees were held in a corner of two jails for several years, in a twilight zone of legality, without work and recreation, with little contact with their families and no prospect of a release. In the women's camp, the women wailed continuously, as though in mourning, the team wrote in its report.

Men, women and children above six were each separated from the members of their families. Many had not met their spouse for several years, many not even once since their detention, given that women and men were in different jails, and they never were given parole or permission to come together. Children who turned six were sent out to the care of relatives or the community, their future legal status uncertain.

The government made no distinction between these detention centres and jails, but there was no legal regime governing the rights and entitlements of detainees. So even though they were in jail, unlike convicts, they could not get parole or waged work.

The NHRC took no action on the team's findings and Mander quit. Assam's National Register of Citizens (NRC) was released in 2019, and it left out about nineteen lakh individuals.[91] A year later, these nineteen lakh people had still not received written confirmation of their exclusion.[92] This meant that they could not file an appeal though they had been disenfranchised and could not vote. All of them continued to live with thoughts of separation from family. The government of India also told the parliament that only Muslims would be kept in the camps and non-Muslims would be freed.[93]

116 The Anarchist Cookbook

This was the future that awaited India's Muslims if the BJP brought in the nationwide NRC. They were goaded and forced into protest by a State intent on molesting them through the citizenship law. On 11 December, the Citizenship (Amendment) Act (CAA) was passed.

Home Minister Amit Shah said that the law was to be read in conjunction with the National Register of Citizens. The CAA would identify and protect non-Muslims, after which the NRC would come for the Muslims.

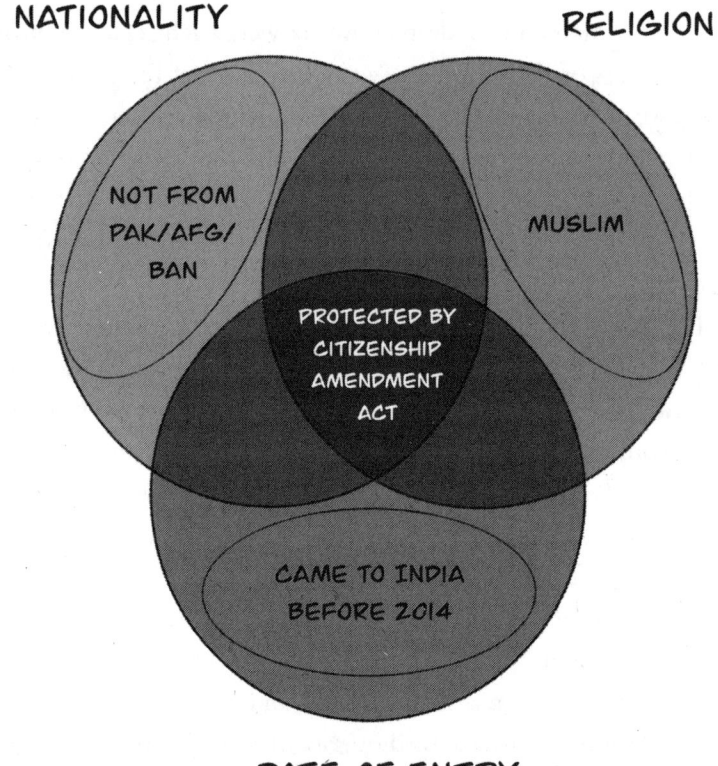

There was no resistance from the polity on this, including from the Opposition. If India's Muslims did not stand up for their rights, they would be brutalized while others looked on. They chose to make a stand in a spontaneous moment that defined Modi's second term, gave Indians hope and a model for peaceful resistance, drew the admiration of the world and, most importantly, finished off the idea of a nationwide NRC.

On the night of 15 December 2019, angered by the police violence against the students of Jamia who were peacefully protesting the passage of the CAA, the residents of Shaheen Bagh sat out in the winter cold to announce their resistance. The road they occupied was a part of GD Birla Marg, which connected Delhi with Uttar Pradesh. This was a Muslim neighbourhood and it would not be easy for the police which functioned under the jurisdiction of the Ministry of Home Affairs, headed by Amit Shah at the time, to storm the area and just boot them off the road. Also, the protest was led by and mostly populated by Shaheen Bagh's women, which further complicated potential use of force.

The protest grew quickly in size—and in significance and influence. It was simple enough to replicate as a model. India's Muslims are forced to live in urban ghettos. They were, therefore, the majority in these neighbourhoods and felt safe in them. Muslim women, many of whom rarely left their homes, could come down the road in their neighbourhood and occupy it to announce their protest and participation in the movement.

The Shaheen Bagh model was that of a fixed site, continually occupied, showing unbroken resistance. It had a time-table of cultural activity which made it easy for many to participate. There were performances, speeches, music and lectures through the day and late into the night. The women slept at the protest site. In the morning, a few of them occupied the site in turns. The women attracted solidarity. Fraternity shows itself most visibly, most meaningfully, in protests when those who are not directly concerned join hands and stand up for those who are.

If you felt strongly about the violations and the prejudice in the law, and wanted to express solidarity, or even if you were merely curious, there was a place in your city or town you could go and participate in the resistance. For those who attended and took part, one striking thing was that the movement lost no momentum with time. It could be said with accuracy that the opposite happened. More cities, more students, more universities and more people joined in with time. This required the individuals at each protest site to very quickly learn new skills. They learned how to engage with the State and with the police, to mobilize and control groups, to organize events, to manage the media and to use social media effectively, and how to communicate, to raise money and to erect and maintain a stage or protest site.

Though there were over two hundred sites modelled on Shaheen Bagh across India and in all of its cities (several cities had more than one site), the original remained the focus. It radiated defiance because of the road it had blocked. This was merely an irritant—there were alternative routes between Delhi and UP. But Muslims defying Modi in the capital of India was intolerable. The government tried, and failed, to dislodge the protesters. The movement instead spread and gained credibility.

The Shaheen 'Baghis'—a pun that also means rebels—did not move, even when threatened by an individual brandishing a gun. They were inspirational in a way that no other group of urban protesters had been in India's history. Millions marched across India in protests that were linked to Shaheen Bagh. Their slogan was simple: *Kagaz nahin dikhayenge* (we will not show you our papers).

Once the masses showed themselves, the polity finally acted. West Bengal, on 17 December, and Kerala on 20 December, had already halted the collection of data for the National Population Register (NPR) because of protests which had begun even before the passage of the laws. In the Northeast, especially Assam, there was intense hostility to the idea of the CAA. But it was Shaheen Bagh which made the protests a national movement and an international story. In September 2020, *Time* magazine named Shaheen Bagh granny

Bilkis Bano one of the 100 most influential individuals in the world. The eighty-two-year-old 'became the symbol of resistance in a nation where the voices of women and minorities were being systematically drowned out', the article said.[94]

On 15 January 2020, Kerala challenged the constitutionality of the CAA in the Supreme Court. By this time, it was clear that the movement had succeeded and there would be no NRC. The government also put CAA itself on hold, after the world rallied in support of protesters and a resolution condemning it was moved in Europe's parliament.

On 24 March, with the pandemic restrictions, the Shaheen Bagh protest was vacated. But it had done the job, and more.

Lessons we learned: The No CAA, No NPR, No NRC movement produced a generation of talented mobilizers and organizers. Along with the invention of a workable and effective model of protest, this was the other contribution that the movement has made. Hundreds of young women and men, most of them in their twenties, were now activists with experience of how to manage a group of two hundred or more people, how to raise resources and distribute provisions, how to represent themselves before the media, how to spread the word and expand the protest, how to respond on social media, and so on. They learned how to campaign.

It is true that the moment produced the movement. The collective anguish that was felt by the community made it easier to transform potential energy into action. But collective anguish of its own does not always automatically create a movement. It is important to note that it began with a small group and even perhaps just a couple of individuals who decided that they needed to act. And once a core group made itself visible, it became the centre of the movement.

From that point, the mechanical functions of a protest movement followed. Organizing water and food, shortlisting personalities to invite to the next day's function, reaching out to them on social media—all these became a task. The energy within the group increased as it became bigger, more prominent and arrived on the national news. All of these things happened, but they happened because a core group of a few individuals first decided that they had to act. And act now.

14

'I Can't Breathe'
(Black Lives Matter, 2020)

Black Lives Matter (BLM) was the largest protest movement in American history, a *New York Times* report said in July 2020. One crore people, possibly even two crore, took part in the protests. It was also one of the most effective. It transformed in a matter of weeks the opinion that a majority of white Americans held about their police's treatment of the Black community.

Through May and June 2020, there were over two hundred and sometimes over three hundred daily protests across the US. Events such as these blooded a new generation of activists, gave them the opportunity to learn how to campaign and created a framework in cities where activists and like-minded people could come together and be more effective.

Public opinion in favour of #BLM and its demands shifted by more than 25 per cent points, an incredible feat achieved by the protesters in a nation where opinions do not easily change.

The mobilization by the protesters linked up with other movements and helped spread voter awareness, leading to the defeat of Donald Trump in 2020 in crucial states like Georgia.

The #BLM story began in 2013, when three women—Alicia Garza, Patrisse Cullors and Opal Tometi—created a Black-centred movement in response to the acquittal of the murderer of a young Black man, Trayvon Martin.

In May 2020, George Floyd, a forty-six-year-old Black man, died in Minneapolis after a white policeman handcuffed him, pinned him to the ground, and kneeled on his neck for more than eight minutes. Bystanders captured videos of Floyd repeatedly saying, 'I can't breathe,' but policeman George Chauvin did not lift his knee. Floyd died. The next day, after the video went viral, the Minneapolis police chief fired all four men involved in the arrest.

While this was not the first time such an event had been captured on video—and certainly not the first time that a white policeman had brutalized a Black man—it was a trigger. Millions, Black, white and Asian, came out on the streets. While there was some violence because of the sheer number of people involved, the vast majority of the protests were peaceful. They were also innovative. One of the ways of demonstrating involved thousands of protesters lying on the ground chanting 'I can't breathe.' This, along with the Black Lives Matter cry, became the slogan of the movement. The protests climaxed on Juneteenth—the nineteenth of June, when the abolition of slavery is celebrated.

Minneapolis legislators sided with BLM and moved to disband the city's police department. The state's governor also promised urgent reform. In New York, the mayor said the state would prioritize the police's work and focus on youth and social services, key issues for the Black community. California, Nevada, Texas and Washington DC banned their police from ever using chokeholds. Many states also accelerated the process of publicly releasing footage from the body-cameras all police officers carried. Dallas implemented a new order instructing officers 'to either stop, or attempt to stop, another employee when force is being inappropriately applied or is no longer required.'[95]

The police were also required to use car dashboard cameras. A new database was set up to collect video footage documenting police violence at the demonstrations. Activists put out a public spreadsheet documenting five hundred incidents of police brutality. This spreadsheet helped the public locate videos from their neighbourhoods. This was significant and meaningful change.

Another significant impact these demonstrations had was the toppling of several statues of persons linked to slavery and the Confederacy. These monuments to hatred and racism had for long been defended as the heritage of the US. Statues of Christopher

Columbus were taken down in Minnesota, Boston, Miami and thirty other places. Columbus and his crew had committed unspeakable atrocities on native Americans in their quest to conquer the nation, something that was overlooked in his image of a heroic pioneer. Statues of the slave-owning President Andrew Jackson, Confederate President Jefferson Davis (who led the fight in support of slavery against Abraham Lincoln) and Confederate General Stonewall Jackson were all taken down in Virginia. A statue of a Confederate officer in Alabama that had stood for 120 years was taken down because of BLM. A controversial statue of Abraham Lincoln himself, standing over a newly emancipated Black man, was also taken down in Boston.

The movement spread even to the UK where a statue of slave trader Edward Colston in Bristol was uprooted and dumped in the river.

Many Americans had cheered the taking down of statues of Vladimir Lenin, Joseph Stalin and Saddam Hussein in other nations but were aghast when this happened in their own country. But this was because they had been all along viewing their own history through rose-tinted glasses.

The other changes BLM produced was in the media where the popular show *Cops* (which showed police officers arresting and violently taking down mostly Black men) was cancelled. The pop music band Dixie Chicks removed the word Dixie (denoting the Confederate South) from their name.

The booing and boycott of sportsmen who would take a knee during the traditional playing of the national anthem before games also ended. The practice may have begun with just one lone and hated figure, the football player Colin Kaepernick, who found himself without a team. But by the end of BLM, teams across the world were taking the knee in solidarity with the movement. The

Cleveland Indians, a famous baseball team, said it would drop the word Indians and banned the use of face paint and native American headgear by fans. Another top football team, Kansas City Chiefs, also banned paint and native American headgear.

Mississippi, one of the most conservative states in the US, removed the Confederate emblem from its flag. The state of Rhode Island dropped the words 'and Providence Plantations' from its official name because of the association with slavery. Across the world, including in India, cosmetics companies came under pressure to stop selling 'skin whitening' and 'skin lightening' creams.

All of this happened, quite incredibly, in a matter of just a few days in mid-2020.

Lessons we learned: The protesters received some pushback from the administration, led by the openly prejudiced Donald Trump. But they ploughed on through the weeks leading to the US presidential election, changing the dynamic of the election and introducing their agenda solidly into politics. The protesters pushed candidates to say they would address police violence, and they ensured that they had enough popular support to affect the election. One way in which they did this was through voter registration to ensure that Black voters and BLM supporters could vote. The second aspect was ensuring that there was a high turnout from this set of people for the presidential election of 2020. This became a significant factor in battleground states such as Georgia and Wisconsin. Linking the support that the BLM movement generated to the election ensured that the protest achieved its political goal.

An astonishing nine of every ten voters said the protests over police violence were a factor in their voting, with more than three-fourths calling it a major factor, according to a report in *The New York Times*.[96] One in five voters said the protests were the single-most important factor in their decision at the ballot box. Political success ensured that the outcomes that they were reaching for, namely legislation that made America safer for Black individuals, became possible. For those looking to see how a mass movement can be started and then finished, Black Lives Matter offers an outstanding example. The BLM site (*blacklivesmatter.com/resources/*) has an excellent toolkit for protesters.

But the movement was leaderless and, like Shaheen Bagh, the original group of people were only fellow members of a wider movement that took on a life of its own.

'We fought to change history and we won' was the headline in the BBC when it interviewed the BLM founders. This is quite true.

15

Your Mother, You Take Care of Her
(Dalit Lives Matter, 2016)

Black Lives Matter was about a marginalized group demanding equality and better treatment from the State. Something similar happened in India around the same time as BLM which many around the world, and even many in our own country, may not have known about. It was the successful protest by Gujarat's Dalit community against a government that looked the other way while they were brutalized and denied their rights.

On 11 July 2016, seven Dalit men who were skinning a cow's carcass were assaulted, flogged and humiliated for hours in the town of Una, near the Somnath temple. The police stood by.[97] Videos taken by those who participated in and witnessed the assault were watched by millions over the next few days. This was during a time India was going through a period of madness and extreme street violence over beef. This period began after Prime Minister Narendra Modi's government asked states to legislate laws against beef (cow slaughter had already been banned in these states) and its possession.⁹⁸ Maharashtra and Haryana responded in 2015 and the lynchings began.

Criminalizing possession of meat was problematic because the constitutional instruction on cattle slaughter says it is required for animal husbandry. But in a modern era when cows are bred through artificial insemination, and tractors have long replaced bullocks, what was the farmer to do with the male cattle progeny? This the legislation did not care about. They essentially were religious and communal-minded laws pretending to regulate economic crimes. Criminalizing the possession of beef was dangerous in a nation with poor law and order and a weak State unwilling to prevent street violence. Predictably, mobs went after the weakest and most vulnerable. The victims were mostly Muslims,⁹⁹ but in the instance of Una, a group of Dalit men.

The viral videos motivated and inspired the Dalit community to push back. On 18 July, it was reported that seven Dalit persons attempted to immolate themselves in protest. Another nine made the attempt the following day. One of these men, who had consumed poison, died.

Dalit organizations discovered an effective manner of protest—they brought the carcasses of the dead cows they worked with to their protests. These carcasses were dumped outside government offices and on top of government vehicles.

On 18 July, in Surendranagar in central Gujarat, 250 kilometres from Una, Dalit community members brought fifteen trucks of cattle carcasses right outside the Collector's office.¹⁰⁰ This was shocking for people from the dominant castes. They had not seen dead animals on this scale before because the work of skinning and cleaning carcasses was always done in Dalit areas.

'She's your mother, you take care of her,' the Dalit protesters said as they repeated this act across towns and cities in Gujarat.

Of course, no gaurakshak was around to clean up what he had all this time pretended to revere. The Surendranagar Collectorate said it was forced to bury eighty cow carcasses because there was nobody who could usefully strip them as Dalit people did. 'The Dalit community, which usually skins the dead animals and then disposes of the carcass, has been on a strike in the district for one week, so we told the municipal staff to dispose of the dead animals,' Collector Udit Agarwal said.[101]

During these protests, Dalit groups were led by those who had never protested before, including a Dalit businessman, Hirabhai Chawda, who traded in cattle carcass by-products. Till these protests began, many mainstream media organizations remained uninterested in the Una story and the plight of Gujarat's Dalit community. After they took up the Una assault, the results showed immediately. The chief minister finally met the families of the flogging victims.

The turbulence produced new leaders, including the thirty-five-year-old activist and former journalist Jignesh Mevani, who became a lawyer. He likened the actions of those who had attempted suicide to the 2004 protest by Manipuri women against sexual assault by the Armed Forces. The women had protested naked outside Imphal's Kangla Fort—the headquarters of the Assam Rifles—with banners that read 'Indian army rape us'.

'Those women had to strip naked and say, "Indian army rape us" in order for the nation to pay attention to their plight,' Mevani said. 'The suicide attempts are similar.'[102]

In August, Mevani mobilized thousands of people for a four hundred kilometre march from Ahmedabad to Una. He used the momentum to push for material changes, primarily by picking up the issue of surplus land, which had been taken from the feudal landowners by the law but not redistributed to Dalits as it should have been.

In 2006, 115 landless Dalit families of Saroda village near Ahmedabad were allotted 222 bighas (around 136 acres, or about 1.1 acres per family) of land under the Agriculture Land Ceiling Act. The possession, however, was only on paper. The land had been encroached upon by people from the dominant caste. The Dalit families had made representations to the government to no effect.

Mevani picked up the issue, which also touched others from the community in Gujarat, and ensured the allotment of more than 56,000 acres, forcefully. His slogan was: '*Gai nu puchdu tamey rakho, amne amaari jameen aapo* (Keep the cow's tail for yourself and give us our land).[103]

On 8 August, with protests building, Prime Minister Modi was moved to respond by saying that Hindutva vigilantes should kill him rather than attacking Dalit 'brothers'.[104] This response spurred the protesters as they continued their agitation.

In September, a 'rail roko' was announced when Modi was to visit Gujarat to celebrate his sixty-sixth birthday. The agitation was planned at Maninagar, Modi's former constituency, and the threat goaded the state government into engaging with a group it had previously been contemptuous of. The home minister made an assurance that the demands on land would be met. On 20 September, the government began mapping land at Saroda.[105]

Two days later, the state government announced the setting up of sixteen special courts for swiftly completing trials of cases under the Scheduled Caste and Scheduled Tribe (Prevention of Atrocities) Act.[106]

Courts would be set up in fifteen districts, with Ahmedabad getting two. Anand, Banaskantha, Bharuch, Bhavnagar, Gandhinagar, Jamnagar, Junagadh, Kutch, Mehsana, Patan, Rajkot, Surat, Surendranagar and Vadodara would get the rest. The state's notification said the courts were being established after consultation with the chief justice of Gujarat High Court. This had been a long-standing Dalit demand that was fulfilled only on the back of the community's protests after Una.

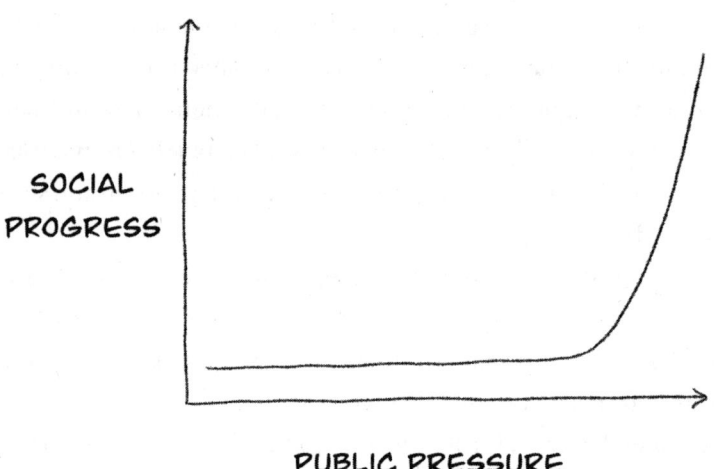

On 1 October, the courts began functioning. The first conviction came five months later, on 25 March 2017, for a case registered in 2013. Conviction rates under the SC/ST Act had been dropping before this. In 2012, a total of 1,026 cases were registered but ended in only sixty-five convictions. In 2015, a mere eleven convictions ensued from the 1,009 cases registered.[107]

One of the reasons for the delay in disposal of cases was the high number of judge vacancies. At the beginning of 2013, Gujarat had the highest number of vacancies (794) in all of India.

In December 2017, only seventeen months after the events of Una, Mevani was elected to the Gujarat Assembly, having become a nationally recognised figure. He remains prominent today, an active voice of resistance who represents the Dalit community.

Lessons we learned: What are our takeaways from this civil rights victory? The proximate cause of the movement was the violence and assault in Una. But behind this lay a deeper sentiment. The Dalits of Gujarat had always felt anguish about their condition in society, their treatment, the discrimination and the daily humiliations. This movement focused their trauma on a fixed set of outcomes and used its energy to achieve them. On the face of it, the brutality on the issue of cattle slaughter, equity in land distribution and the setting up of additional courts appear unrelated issues. But clearly, they were not.

Protests often have an umbrella nature with a set of people who need dissimilar concerns redressed, usually by the State. Good activists are able to bring them together and widen their movement.

16

This Land Is My Land
(Pathalgadi, 2016)

Like the Dalits, the Adivasis of India are a community which is vulnerable and exploited. While atrocious laws like the Coal Bearing Areas Act (which we discuss on p. 200) have existed for decades, there have been some safeguards that protect the Adivasi areas.

The Fifth Schedule of the Indian Constitution provides for special administration of tribal areas, specifically to prevent the alienation of Adivasis from their lands. No land in these areas can be transferred to non-Adivasis.

In Jharkhand, this protection came from the Santhal Pargana Tenancy Act (SPTA) governing the eastern part of the state and the Chotanagpur Tenancy Act (CTA). Both laws were written by the British. The first after the Santhal rebellion of 1855, the second, in 1908, after the rebellion by Birsa Munda. Munda died fighting the British in 1900 at the age of twenty-five, but the British conceded the protections to the Adivasi people. After 1947, both laws remained to restrict the sale and transfer of Adivasi land to non-Adivasis.

In November 2015, the BJP government in Jharkhand approved a plan to expand the capital city of Ranchi. This would involve acquiring 39,000 acres of fertile land—and making thousands of Adivasis landless. Right to Information (RTI) responses revealed that in seven villages which had a total available land of 3,200 acres, the government would take 2,200 acres and the Central Industrial Security Force would take another 158 acres.

The background to this was that Jharkhand's towns like Ranchi, Dhanbad and Bokaro were not planned; they just sprang up. Nine of ten homes in Ranchi had been built without clearance, the government told Jharkhand High Court in 2011.

The number of towns in the state grew from thirteen in 1901 to thirty-five in 1951 and to 228 in 2011. The urban population of the state went from 2 per cent in 1901 to 24 per cent in 2011.[108]

In 2016, the BJP passed amendments to the SPTA and CTA. A fifth of all land in the state had already been acquired for mining and dams, displacing forty lakh Adivasis.

The party was led by Jharkhand's first non-Adivasi chief minister, Raghubar Das. The changes in the laws, first through ordinance in May and then through the legislature in November, would enable the government to acquire Adivasi land for non-agriculture use. At its discretion the government could acquire land for things 'like road, canal, railway, cable transmission, pipelines, and schools, colleges, universities, panchayat buildings, hospitals, anganwadis' as well as any other 'government purpose' notified in the gazette. The ordinances were opposed by Stan Swamy, whom readers will be familiar with as one of those jailed in the Bhima Koregaon case and who died without getting bail on 5 July 2021 (the targeting of activists by the State in India through fake, cooked up and reckless allegations is quite deliberate and naked and common).[109] 'The extension of the listed use and intended purposes in sub-section 49(1)(C) are clearly for real estates, educational institutes and hospitals under private or PPP model,' Swamy had said.[110]

According to Swamy, the Jharkhand chief minister had said at an investment roadshow in Mumbai that the changes in law would make available 71,000 hectares (1,75,000 acres) to industry.

At a Make in India event earlier in the year, Das had signed agreements with industrialists for investments of ₹62,000 crore, with the Adani group alone accounting for ₹50,000 crore.[111]

In August 2016, the National Commission for Scheduled Tribes said the amendments violated two Central laws including the Panchayat Extension to Scheduled Areas Act, which required the taking of consent from gram sabhas when land was transferred.

On 23 October, as it was clear that the ordinances would become law, the Adivasi people rebelled and said they would not stand for the changes. Into a crowd of Munda tribal protesters, the same community Birsa had come from, the police fired eleven rounds, killing an elder, Abhram Mundu.

In January 2017, tribal people protesting against the laws hurled shoes at the chief minister. By July, after sustained opposition, Draupadi Murmu, the governor of Jharkhand, returned the laws with questions. A former BJP minister, who was from the Santhal community herself, cited 192 protest petitions she had received against the laws and asked the government to explain how the changes would help the people.

The Constitution's Fifth Schedule gives special powers to the governor to safeguard Adivasi rights and ensure legislation is aligned with their customary laws and social and religious practices. The executive, however, was usually able to avoid this provision and have its way. Adivasi participation in decision making remained limited.

As the protests against the changes in the land laws were unfolding, the Adivasis began to assert their rights more openly. They erected stone monoliths, called pathals, outside their villages which

- declared their gram sabha as the sovereign authority;
- banned 'outsiders' from their area;
- asserted that Adivasis were the real inhabitants of this land: 'Jal, jangal, jameen (water, forest and land) is ours and no one can take them away from us';
- said that 'voter IDs and Aadhaar cards are anti-Adivasi documents';
- reproduced Article 13(3) which defines a law as any 'custom or usage having in the territory of India the force of law'. This was taken to mean that existing Adivasi custom or law as defined by the village gram sabha (so far as it did not violate the constitution) had the force of the constitution;
- reproduced excerpts from the Panchayats (Extension to Scheduled Areas) Act, 1996, which gave them special rights over managing their affairs in accordance with custom and tradition. And to safeguard and preserve their cultural identity, community resources, and the customary mode of dispute resolution; and
- reproduced court judgments which supported what they were saying.[112]

Some of these stone tablets stood around fifteen feet tall and four feet wide, painted in green with white lettering. As more Adivasi villages began to do this, the action took on the nature of a movement called Pathalgadi, or the erecting of Pathals. Some villages had put them up a few years earlier, but most came up because of the recent laws. By September 2017, over 200 villages had erected them.

On 17 August 2017, a police officer was not allowed to leave a village. Why should we allow outsiders to enter into our villages, they asked, 'when the peace is disturbed, the police come and brand us Naxals and beat us up for no reason'.

In 2018, the bodyguards of a former member of parliament were held by Pathalgadi supporters, who wanted their people to be released by the police.

The Adivasis demanded that funds earmarked for tribal plans should be distributed to the gram sabhas; that the amendments to the land acquisition bills should be scrapped; and that all police and paramilitary camps should be withdrawn from the Scheduled Areas.

The BJP government responded by filing mass FIRs against the Adivasis, including for sedition. In just one district, Khunti, the administration booked 11,400 individuals, including more than 10,000 for sedition, between July 2017 and July 2018.[113] This was 2 per cent of the population of Khunti, which was where Birsa Munda was from.

The Jharkhand Janadhikar Mahasabha, a network of social movements and organisations, sent a fact-finding team of activists, academics and lawyers to Khunti. They found that 'the state responded to Pathalgadi with severe repression and violence. Adivasis in some villages were severely beaten, houses were raided and ransacked. In Ghaghra village, a pregnant woman, Ashrita Munda, delivered a physically disabled baby, a couple of weeks after being beaten by the police during a raid.'[114]

Their report said that 'the police has also forcefully set up camps in schools and community buildings without the consent of gram sabhas in many Adivasi villages.'

The resistance from the Adivasis was one of the key issues the Opposition used to win the elections that came in 2019. In December 2019, before voting, the Jharkhand Mukti Morcha said it would drop the cases if it came to power. After its leader Hemant Soren became chief minister, he announced the dropping of all Pathalgadi cases of 2017 and 2018. The new Cabinet's first decision was to drop the sedition cases.

A year later, about two-thirds of the cases had been withdrawn.

Lessons we learned: The Pathalgadi agitation, a sustained mass movement that many Indians outside Jharkhand did not know about, achieved a comprehensive citizenry victory over the State. And that too by a set of people with no voice in the national media, with no external spotlight on their efforts and no allies other than their own. Truly a case of David felling Goliath.

Not only did they force the government to roll back the offending laws but defeated the party that wrote them and got most of the cases against them withdrawn. What a terrific story it is and, like Shaheen Bagh, Una, #MeToo and BLM, an inspiration to all protest movements around the world.

17

Never Too Small to Make a Difference
(Fridays for Future, 2016)

At the end of her first week on strike in August 2018, Greta Thunberg handed out flyers that said: 'You grown-ups don't give a shit about my future.'

The next year she was nominated for the Nobel Peace Prize, something that would happen again in 2020 and in 2021.

The eighteen-year-old rose to lead a millions-strong youth movement demanding action on global warming. They did this through an innovative action—called Fridays For Future (FFF)—by refusing to go to school on Fridays.

On 20 August 2018, when she was fifteen, Thunberg skipped school and held up the signs of her protest outside Sweden's parliament. The next week, she was joined not just by fellow students but teachers and parents. This brought the attention of the media in a part of the world that is feeling and is aware about the effects of climate change.

From the next month, Thunberg made the Friday strikes a regular feature. She invited students to walk out of their classroom and schools and come to protest sites. Their demand was that politicians take the issue more seriously and act immediately to secure the future of those they were imperiling through inaction on climate change.

By November, more than 17,000 students in two dozen nations were regularly taking part in FFF strikes. Thunberg, a good public speaker despite her age, was invited to high profile events across Europe. This included the United Nations' climate talks in Poland. By the beginning of the following year, FFF took on even more momentum and spread to places as far from Sweden as India and

Brazil. FFF empowered a group of us who usually have no power and no say, even about their own future.

Thunberg's response to her first Nobel Prize nomination, and the resultant praise from adults, was that of scorn. They should be saying what she was, she would tell them, instead of applauding her as if she was saying something they didn't know. By now, the number of students taking part in FFF reached over twenty lakh a week across 135 nations. In May of 2019, *Time* magazine named Thunberg one of the world's most influential people and put her on the cover. 'Now I am speaking to the whole world', Thunberg wrote on Twitter. And indeed, by now she had become easily one of the most influential and perhaps the most influential voice globally on the issue of climate change.

She received some pushback from conservative and far-right politicians (including Donald Trump) because they favoured a slow approach to legislation curbing emissions and more freedom for the fossil fuel industry.

On 31 January 2019, more than 3,400 Belgian scientists and academics signed an open letter in support of the FFF strikes. They said: 'On the basis of the facts supplied by climate science, the campaigners are right. That is why we, as scientists, support them.'[115]

This was followed by a letter of support from the Netherlands, signed by 340 scientists, and another by 1,200 researchers in Finland. An article published in the highly respected *Nature* magazine quoted scientists hailing the FFF movement as the right form of non-violent civil disobedience.[116]

FFF inspired a group of scientists in Germany, Austria and Switzerland to found Scientists for Future (S4F) in support of the facts being promoted by FFF.

Thunberg carried on her work and in August of 2019 assembled 450 young climate activists across Europe to plan the movement's development. By that month, the total number of FFF strikers in schools reached thirty six lakh, now in more than 169 nations.[117]

She sailed to the US (preferring not to fly because of airline carbon emissions) taking fourteen days to participate in a UN summit on climate change. She also protested outside the White House, especially because Trump had threatened to pull the US out of the Paris Agreement under which nations voluntarily undertook cuts in greenhouse gas emissions. This would ensure that the rise in global temperatures would be no more than two degrees centigrade over what they had been in the times before the industrial revolution. Trump did pull the US out, but President Joe Biden brought America in again.

Invited to speak to a US Congressional hearing, Thunberg delivered a blistering speech and said that the world's leaders had 'stolen my dreams and my childhood with your empty words'. Who could deny this, given what continues to happen all around us? Soon after, she was named the winner of the Right Livelihood Award, also called the alternative Nobel. What began as a lone individual holding a placard had evolved in the shortest time possible into a global movement which the world and its leaders could not ignore.

The movement was not widely known in India till February 2021, when one tweet changed everything. Greta Thunberg tweeted out a toolkit for protest in support of the movement against the three farm laws passed in 2020. The word 'toolkit' was deliberately misconstrued by the media and the government to be some sort of guide to violence. Following this, the founder of FFF in India, twenty-one-year-old Disha Ravi, was arrested. Her jailing was condemned globally, and a court freed her a few days later saying that there was no evidence against her. A host of celebrities and leaders, both Indian and foreign, came out in her support, making her and the climate cause of FFF famous.

Lessons we learned: Like Shaheen Bagh, FFF had a simple, effective and, more importantly, replicable protest model—in this case a global one.

A replicable model is important for movements that are geographically large and spread out. Our lesson here from these protests is an answer to the question: How can we unite people in different places who are concerned about the same issues? How can a large group of people that cannot meet in one place be mobilized for effective action? One way is the replicable model of protest. Once we have thought through and figured out a way to organize ourselves in one place, the lessons can be extended to other places. Of course, something becomes replicable only if it is interesting and effective.

18

Morcha for Change
(Farmer Protests, 2020)

This is the story of the largest protest and the most successful civil rights victory in the democratic world of our time. The story began in June 2020, when India was reeling under the first wave of the pandemic and the effects of the nationwide lockdown were still being felt, the Modi government passed three Ordinances.[118]

An Ordinance is a law that has not been passed by Parliament and is in effect for a short time. After Parliament passes the law, the ordinance becomes ineffective and the law or Act takes effect.

The three Ordinances aimed to fundamentally change the nature of farming in India by reducing the government's role and handing over more power to corporates. This was done by opening up the sale of agricultural produce to private markets which would not have to pay tax. This would be to the disadvantage of the existing mandis—markets run by state governments—which were taxed. Private individuals could get into contracts with farmers merely on the basis of their possessing a PAN card. And any dispute between the trader or corporate and the farmer could not be taken to court. The farmer could only approach the local bureaucrat who would try and settle the issue. In a dispute between a farmer and a corporate, it can be imagined whose side the bureaucrat would take.

The laws affected all farmers. But the vast majority of India's farmers have no surplus produce to sell, whether in the mandis or a private market. Their land is so small and their produce so limited that they eat what they grow.

Consider that in the US farmers make up less than 2 per cent of the workforce and the average farm size is 444 acres. The average US farmer feeds himself and fifty other Americans (and whatever is sent for export).[119] In India, half the total population depends on agriculture as the primary source of their income.[120] This means that the Indian farmer feeds himself and one other person and the average farm size is only two acres.[121] This is the very definition of subsistence farming.

It was primarily the farmers in a few states in the North that have a surplus of grain, meaning they grow enough to sell. And it was in their states that the mandis were most efficiently run and where their grain was procured. (Incidentally, the rice and wheat that is distributed and sold through the PDS/ration shops comes from these farmers, who essentially feed India's poor.) And it is these farmers who stood in protest immediately after the ordinances were drawn up. They understood what the laws meant for their livelihood and even for the country as a whole.

Why were the laws passed as ordinances on 5 June 2020, when the lockdown had just ended? Why could they not await the opening of parliament?

In September, Parliament passed the legislation and they became law, but a division vote in Rajya Sabha was disallowed, meaning that they were passed without real legitimacy.[122]

The Shiromani Akali Dal, an ally of the BJP for four decades, left the National Democratic Alliance saying it could not support the laws. While India was unaware or distracted, a massive protest began in Punjab which farmers sustained all the way to the borders of Delhi. They were joined by their counterparts from Haryana and Uttar Pradesh, who, too, blocked different border points of Delhi. This is a common tactic of disruption and civil disobedience that even political parties follow in India.

The protesters, owing their allegiance to some forty-odd farming unions, came together to form a single umbrella body, the Samyukta Kisan Morcha (SKM), or United Farmers Front. Thirty-two of these unions came from Punjab and about half of their members were from a single group, led by a former soldier named Joginder Singh from the village of Ugrahan in the district of Sangrur. The protesters were on the highway, in a parked convoy of tractors twenty kilometre long, and they spent their nights in the open bed trailers, known as trolleys.

SKM submitted a list of eight demands to the Modi government in the form of a charter and doughtily stuck to them. Their primary demands were that the government repeal the three farm laws, which one, allowed tax-free trade of agricultural produce outside mandis; two, allowed contract farming; and three, amended the Essential Commodities Act, allowing for the hoarding of agricultural produce by traders and corporates. They also wanted a repeal of laws which criminalized the burning of stubble and the withdrawal of a proposal that sought to end power subsidies. Interestingly, they included what might be considered non-farmer demands also in their list, including the elimination of taxes on fuel to align the price of petrol and diesel to international crude prices and the unconditional release those jailed in the Bhima Koregaon case and for the CAA protests.

Further, they wanted the implementation of a proposal (called the Swaminathan Report) that recommended surplus and waste land be given to landless farmers, and also recommended that the farmers be paid more for the grain that the government procured from them, what is called the Minimum Support Price or MSP.

Government surveys showed that the average Indian farmer's income was ₹77,124 in a year, or ₹6,427 per month. Their monthly expenditure is ₹6,223.[123]

These numbers indicate the desperate situation of agriculturists, the majority of India's population. Even in Punjab, where the farmer is said to be better off, the average monthly income of a farm household before expenses was only ₹18,059.

The farmers' demands were not a product of ignorance, as the ruling party tried to portray.[124] They were the result of understanding, at depth, issues that concerned the farmers, their families and their future. Indeed, the farmers had read the three main laws not just individually but also in conjunction to arrive at the government's intent. This, they concluded, was:

- ending the mandis
- weakening the Public Distribution System (PDS)
- loading the legal framework against the farmer by denying access to the justice system (the law said farmers could not move court against a corporate that reneged or defaulted)
- allowing the private sector to engage farmers at the individual level
- decriminalizing the hoarding of grain and creating monopolies

Trade would naturally shift away in time from the mandis, which were taxed and regulated, to the private marketplaces. The government saying it would not end the mandi system, as it did, would not change the trajectory which the farmers saw the laws taking. In places where the mandi system had been ended, private markets had worsened the position of the farmers. Bihar under Nitish Kumar shut down its entire state-run mandi system in 2006. This also put paid to the MSP in the state. Paddy sold for around ₹950 per quintal (100 kilos) in Bihar, while the MSP was ₹1,868.[125]

The average Bihar farmer's monthly income was ₹3,557. By scrapping the mandi system, and abdicating on governance, the state harmed Bihar's farm households.

Farmers did not budge from their position from the first round of talks, held on 1 December 2020, to the last one on 22 January 2021. By now, the Supreme Court had also stayed the implementation of the laws, effectively handing the farmers a victory.

The farmer groups' leadership attended the protests together. The unions that bound them together made mass mobilization easier.

After it made the initial show of defiance, the government began to soften and offered tweaks as a compromise. Private marketplaces would be taxed if the state government wanted; MSP 'would continue'; the laws on stubble and electricity would be taken back; access to the justice system would be given to farmers. The government even agreed to 'suspend' all the laws for eighteen months—effectively killing them because the period after the suspension would be too close to the next Lok Sabha election of 2024. But there was a refusal to officially repeal the laws, to legally guarantee MSP and to accept the Swaminathan formula for arriving at MSP. The first, a repeal of the laws, was not acceptable to Modi because, analysts concluded, it would damage his strongman image, erode the idea that he led a tough administration and produce further mass movements.[126]

If this was accurate, then Modi, having already put the laws away, continued with the charade that they were still alive and looked away as the farmers' protest continued and tens of thousands of people remained on the streets for months, some of them dying.

But, through all this, the Morcha remained firm on its position.

Much was made of the fact that most of the farmers were from Punjab and Haryana and this was, in that sense, not a national, but a regional movement. This was proved wrong by events in 2021, when the largest gatherings against the laws came in Uttar Pradesh and protests were held around the country.

The farmers' reference to the continued distribution of food grains through the PDS system (in point 1) was reemphasized often. This concern was based on reality. As early as 2015, Modi had determined that India spent too much on food security. He asked bureaucrats to prepare a plan that would limit access to subsidized good grains to 40 per cent of the population.[127]

This would be down from the 67 per cent mandated by the Food Security Act of 2013. A quarter of India's people who were receiving the food grains would be left out.

In that year, the government spent ₹1.25 lakh crore on the consumer food subsidy. In 2017-18, it fell to ₹1.05 lakh crore. The slashing came through subterfuge. The budget allocation was 2016-17 and 2018-19 was about 1.4 lakh crore and ₹1.6 lakh crore, but money was not spent.[128]

In 2019-20, the allocation (meaning the grand announcement) was ₹1.92 lakh crore and the actual spend was ₹1.15 lakh crore. Adjusted for inflation and with the population having risen, the cut Modi desired had been achieved and perhaps exceeded.

There was every reason to believe, if one were a farmer, that not only was there a plan behind the farm laws that was aimed at the PDS and the MSP, but that plan was in execution mode. This is why, through the demonization and the harassment, they did not flinch. They negotiated with Modi's ministers in innovative ways: For hours they would not speak but instead hold up placards in response to questions or proposals. 'Yes or No?' read one of them after they were convinced early on that the government was not negotiating in good faith but merely procrastinating with the intent of tiring them out. SKM's leaders had predicted this and, as early as December 2020, said they had come prepared to stay till the summer and beyond.

This book is being written towards the end of 2021 and they are still mobilized. One way that they could do this was that they rotated their presence. Those who left for their village after a few weeks were replaced by others who stayed for a few weeks in turn. The supply lines for food and essentials were robust. And given that they had their own means of transport—the trolley and the tractor—they were self-sufficient in a way few other Indian communities can be.

Importantly, SKM received strong and sustained backing from parliamentarians in the UK and Canada (where there were more Sikhs—eighteen—in the parliament of 338, than in India, which had only thirteen Sikhs in the Lok Sabha).[129] An intervention from Canadian leader Justin Trudeau came on 1 December 2020 when he expressed his concern at what was happening in India. The Modi government called this 'unacceptable interference' and summoned Canada's High Commissioner to tell him that 'such actions, if continued, would have a seriously damaging impact on ties'.[130]

The very next day, Trudeau again spoke of the issue in support of the farmers.

Trudeau would, in fact, raise the matter directly with Modi on a telephone call the two had on 10 February. The Indian briefing on the call did not refer to this. When the Canadians put it out, the Indian foreign ministry spokesman said Trudeau had actually 'commended efforts of government of India to choose path of dialogue.' Just as it had not calibrated what the citizenship laws would elicit as a response abroad, the government did not anticipate the pushback here either. Its attitude was contemptuous and mendacious. The media was told that the farmers were merely intent on acting in a truculent fashion and did not propose anything. This was untrue.

As early as 1 December 2020, SKM wrote up a draft law which said every farmer throughout India will be entitled to a Guaranteed Remunerative MSP (GRMSP) against the sale of any agricultural commodity.[131]

To understand the context: at present, across all agricultural markets in India, including the Agricultural Produce Market Committees, the auction price for any agricultural commodity begins at the 'floor' price. Meaning that the auction would not be allowed below that price.

SKM's draft proposed that no trader, including one who entered into a contract farming agreement, could purchase an agricultural commodity below the GRMSP, and to do so would be to commit a cognizable offence. The GRMSP would be arrived at by a new body, the Central Farmers Agricultural Costs and Remunerative Price Guarantee Commission. GRMSP would be based on C2, adding 50 per cent as margin.

The Modi government had misread the issue. They had no understanding of the farmers' resolve and what a movement like this would bring in its wake. An early sign that this was not any ordinary protest was that unusual eighth point of the SKM charter. The text reads: 'Unconditional release of arrested pro-democracy intellectuals and anti-CAA activists. Stop suppressing dissent.'

Why would protesters on the subcontinent, where power is skewed disproportionately away from the citizenry and towards the State, insert demands unrelated to their movement? Why would they do this particularly with a government that prided itself in demonizing those who said such things and those who stood in their support?

Because SKM believed in the things it was asking for. It may interest readers to know that all thirty-two of the Punjab farmers' groups signed on to the entire charter, including this demand, which was added to the charter in the very first internal meeting held in Moga in the third week of September. The farmers also raised their demand for the release of the activists in their meeting with Union Agriculture Minister Narendra Singh Tomar in November.

Through the protests, the farmers warmly accepted the support they got from abroad and were never defensive about it. When individuals backing them got into trouble, SKM's support for them was full-throated. One such individual was the young climate change activist Disha Ravi, whom we have talked about earlier. The action was spun to be a global conspiracy against Modi and India. But the farmer leadership did not feel the need to be defensive and stood with her and others. This also encouraged political parties to stand by Indians being abused with the usual slander in the usual sections of the mass media.[132]

On 10 December, Human Rights Day, the Tikri site held an event featuring the photographs of Gautam Navlakha, Varavara Rao, Sudha Bharadwaj, Vernon Gonsalves, Arun Ferreira, Umar Khalid and others jailed in the Bhima Koregaon case and for the CAA protests on the stage.

'What did people like Gautam Navlakha or Sudha Bharadwaj do? They showed how poor people in remote areas are living under extreme stress and how they were unfairly treated by the governments. There are others who show how people of Kashmir live in constant fear of the security forces. We believe that the Modi government put all of them in prison only to silence them. It is our responsibility, then, to speak up for the citizens,' Joginder Singh Ugrahan said.

Events towards the end of 2020 and beginning of 2021 reveal with clarity that the laws were not going to be implemented.

First, on 12 January, a three-judge bench headed by Chief Justice of India S.A. Bobde said the Supreme Court was 'extremely disappointed' with the way the Modi government was handling the issue.[133] On 13 January the court 'stayed' the laws (it was uncertain what this meant because no legal ground was given).[134] The media reported that the government was relieved as this gave it a way out without having officially surrendered to the farmers. The stay addressed points 1, 2 and 3 of the charter.[135]

The court also set up a committee of four individuals, all of whom had publicly expressed support for the farm laws, to 'evaluate' them and submit a report within two months. This report came in a sealed cover at the end of March 2021, but its findings were not revealed.[136]

And finally, the government itself undid its repeal of the Essential Commodities Act on 2 July, by limiting how much dal traders could hoard. This was the last nail in the coffin because it meant that the laws were not being implemented. And yet the farmers continued their protest because once demobilized, it would not be easy to redeploy thousands on the ground. They had little faith in the polity's ability to stand up for them once their resistance on the street had dissipated. It is this courage of theirs that carried the day for India's farmers. On the morning of 19 November 2021, the prime minister appeared on television to announce the repeal of the laws and to apologize to the nation. Thus concluded after a year, this protest, the result of sustained mass mobilization, clarity of message, doggedness and the campaigning spirit. Truly one of the significant moments of democracy and peaceful resistance in history.

Lessons we learned: It is only sustained mass protest that moves the Indian state. When mass mobilization happens and remains on the field, the State retreats. And the Kisan Morcha was the most striking example of that in our time.

Like the women of Shaheen Bagh, the farmers recognized that gaining visibility for their message was paramount. They succeeded strikingly in getting noticed around the world. Right at the beginning, aware of the reality of media in India, they began a newspaper of their own, *Trolley Times*, circulated at the protest sites. They also opened social media accounts and began to broadcast live the events from the stages they had erected on the highway. They attracted support internationally. Their cause—the hardy peasant standing up to corporate greed—was popular and their protest both massive and striking. Celebrities jumped in and discovered how vicious the social media space in India is. Tweets from the singer Rihanna, climate activist Greta Thunberg and porn star Mia Khalifa became front page news and also, more ridiculously, earned them finger-wagging lectures from Union Minister S. Jaishankar's Foreign Ministry and pious and identical responses from Indian celebrities like Sachin Tendulkar (who tweeted: 'India's sovereignty cannot be compromised. External forces can be spectators but not participants. Indians know India and should decide for India. Let's remain united as a nation. #IndiaTogether #IndiaAgainstPropaganda') and Akshay Kumar, who were among those retweeting the government's pushback. But this only showed that what the farmers had achieved in controlling the narrative. A great lesson in putting one's message out.

19

A Lost Battle
(ASHAs, 2020)

We have so far looked at protests that have worked, in the sense that they have either achieved their objective—such as in the case of Una, Pathalgadi and No NRC—or made substantial progress on an issue which was not in the public eye—such BLM and #MeToo. But there are other protests that did not find similar success despite mobilizing large numbers of people.

The reality is that unless mass mobilization is sustained, the State does not engage with citizens in our part of the world. It doesn't matter if the cause is just and of a pressing nature. It doesn't matter even if it is something vital for the nation and its citizens. If it can be ignored because it is not seen as politically important, it will likely be. This is the story of such a group of people. If you have not read or known about them or their demands before, it is because this does not make the mainstream media which is focused on other, irrelevant and often demented, things.

In August 2020, at the height of the pandemic's first wave, six lakh Accredited Social Health Activists (ASHAs) went on a two-day strike. They demanded the same protection from Covid-19 as doctors, health insurance and better and timely compensation. These were frontline workers, 'Covid warriors' valorized by Narendra Modi—who were sent out to battle with no PPE kits, sanitizers, masks or gloves.

These, grassroots workers employed under the Centre's National Health Mission, have the following responsibilities:[137]

- Create awareness and provide information on nutrition, sanitation and hygiene.
- Counsel women on birth preparedness, safe delivery, breast-feeding, immunization, contraception and prevention of common infections.
- Work with the Village Health & Sanitation Committee of the Gram Panchayat to develop a comprehensive village health plan.
- Escort/accompany pregnant women and children to the nearest health centre.
- Provide primary medical care for minor ailments such as diarrhoea, fevers, and first aid for injuries, the short course for tuberculosis.
- Supervise storage of essential provisions being made available to every habitation including oral rehydration salts (ORS), iron folic acid tablets, chloroquine, disposable delivery kits and contraceptives like pills and condoms.

They are not paid a salary but receive some compensation, a part of which may or may not be fixed by the state they work in. They receive small incentives for completing recurring tasks like updating

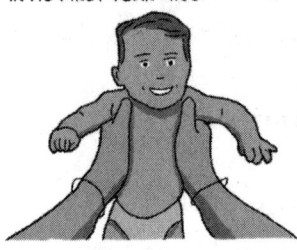

the lists of children to be immunized. For all the work they do, they stand to make only between ₹2,000 and ₹4,500 a month.[138]

ASHAs are aged between twenty-five and forty-five and literate, having studied up to class ten.

During the pandemic, many ASHAs worked fourteen hours a day, documenting people's quarantine schedules and tracking their districts for influenza-like symptoms. And they were the ones called upon for vaccinating the rural Indian population.

In Delhi, ASHAs are paid ₹4,000 a month. All they asked for was ₹10,000. Their protest in Jantar Mantar—the 'designated area' where causes go to die —went unheard. In fact, 100 of the 'Covid warriors' were booked. Women who had been force-marched to the frontline of the pandemic with no protection faced the charge, brought by Delhi Police, of 'violating social distancing norms'. In Bihar, many of the state's nearly ninety thousand ASHAs went on strike in August 2020. Several had not been paid for four months. Some had contracted Covid-19 on the job.

In Karnataka, many ASHAs had not been paid for a year. They had not even been paid the ₹1,000 the state government said it would give them for Covid-related work. The workers went on strike twice, in August and September 2020, but were not able to even secure a meeting with the state health minister.

Gujarat's ASHAs had not received their dues for a year even before Covid-19. About three thousand women in Gir Somnath, Porbandar and Junagadh districts went on strike for about ten days leading up to Women's Day on 8 March 2019. Back in 2017, they had withdrawn another strike after being assured a 50 per cent hike. Later, they discovered that the 'hike' had been accompanied by a withdrawal of other benefits—so there was no increase at all. They did not even make ₹3,000 a month.

ASHAs in Madhya Pradesh went on strike even earlier, in 2018. They protested for over ten days in October seeking a fixed salary and permanent employment. The state would pay them between ₹800 and ₹1,000 per month besides other 'incentives' such as ₹250 for nine months' antenatal care resulting in an institutional delivery.

In Haryana, twenty thousand ASHAs struck work on 7 August 2020 and then again in October, demanding implementation of the health department's assurance of regularization—an assurance made on 21 July 2018. They also sought incentives for services and risk allowances during the pandemic.

In Rajasthan, they had struck work for days in September 2017, seeking more than the ₹1,850 they received from the state. They struck work again at the end of 2020, dissatisfied with the renaming of their job title to ASHA Sahayogini and the merging of incentives that resulted in a pay of around ₹2,700. In January 2021, Chief Minister Ashok Gehlot wrote to Prime Minister Modi seeking more money for the state's 52,000 ASHAs, saying that there had been no hike in the incentives payable by the Centre for their work.

Even in Kerala, they were not on the vaccine priority list despite being 'frontline warriors'.

In Punjab, ASHAs went on a hunger strike for the restoration of a monthly Covid-19 'incentive' of ₹2,500 that had been reduced in June 2020 to ₹1,000.

They would only be paid the ₹1,000 if the population they catered to was above the poverty line. The incentive was higher if the population was predominantly poor—but that came with significant risks such as dealing with patients who had tuberculosis.

Another issue these ASHAs faced was the lack of a smartphone in which they were supposed to enter household Covid-19 survey data.

Of the 21,500 ASHAs in Punjab, around fifteen thousand had no smartphones. They had to borrow these from friends and relatives just to go about their work. They were paid ₹4 per person whose data they uploaded.[139]

If the government triples what the around ten lakh ASHAs in India are paid on an average and gave them ₹12,000 a month, it would still be only entail a cost of around ₹10,000 crores a year. Surely, that would have been money well spent in a nation of generally poor health, especially amid a pandemic that was hurting it economically.

Despite their resolve, the ASHAs could not move India to do justice with them. Their protest petered out though it was supported by various national trade unions including the INTUC, AITUC, HMS, CITU, AIUTUC, TUCC, SEWA, AICCTU, LPF and UTUC. None of these unions appeared to have the capacity to convert a large problem and tens of thousands of willing agitators into a large scale, national and continuous protest.

Lessons we learned: If more of us as citizens, as people concerned with the pandemic and what it was doing to our society, had stood by the ASHAs, the government would have conceded their just demands. Their inability to get the State to accept even such modest terms as a fixed salary, especially in the time of a pandemic they were being asked to fight against, is also our collective failure. They required us as citizens to: firstly, understand what they did and what they were paid; secondly, to assess their contribution in a time of a pandemic; and thirdly, to nudge government policy towards doing the right thing. We failed them collectively.

For mass protest to work in India, it has to be sustained. If the State is not interested in the issue, has a stake in the issue or is hostile to the protesters, the only way to draw its attention and hold it is through sustained defiance. The State—and especially a government such as Modi's—understands the news cycle. It can deflect, distract or ignore the issue long enough for it to die down due to a lack of enthusiasm, organizational ability or just stamina.

SECTION IV

Lawless Laws

20

Dangerous until Proven Innocent

It is not seen in that way, especially in our part of the world, but the criminal justice system of the civilized world is deliberately designed to protect the rights of the accused. And this is the correct way of seeing it. Why? Because, in a criminal case, there are two parties in adversarial positions. The accused individual and the State. A crime is an offence against the State and not a private wrong. When a theft, assault, murder or fraud happens, the rules by which the State runs the country (rules that we call laws) are violated and it must deliver justice to society. This is unlike in ancient Greece, where a crime was a personal wrong which needed to be avenged or repaired. In the criminal justice system of our time, it is the State that takes on the role of the punisher. It engages with the accused to bring about justice and puts the individual through a process that is the criminal justice system.

But the State controls the rules under which the system operates. It legislates the laws punishing the accused. It appoints, pays the salaries of and manages the police forces who accuse, arrest and investigate. It appoints and pays the prosecutors who will represent it against the individual.

It pays and promotes the judges who determine innocence or guilt.

The State holds all the power. The individual has none.

Most accused in India have no money even to get proper representation and, therefore, a defence against the State.

That is why we have the principle of innocent until proven guilty. The understanding is that the State has overwhelming and terrible power in a criminal case. A conviction, even for a minor offence, has the power to destroy lives permanently.

Even though justice is represented as a blind woman with balanced scales, the scales are not balanced. The state can load as much weight as it wants to on one side.

In India after independence, the State has not been satisfied with the amount of power it has. It has always needed more.

There are few hurdles stopping the State from giving more power to itself except the voters. And voters in India have little interest in the criminal justice system. Most of our club of elite do not think the criminal justice system concerns them. So, the State can give itself whatever sweeping power it wants.

What it wants is to reverse the most fundamental judicial principle to 'guilty until proven innocent'. In India, the State has been giving itself this power to do this.

Laws that Indians protested against when they were being written by the British colonial State can be implemented today by a democratic State, even though their effect on the individual is the same.

This is a power under which the State can arrest individuals without a crime, on the assumption that they may commit a crime in future. This is 'guilty until proven innocent'.

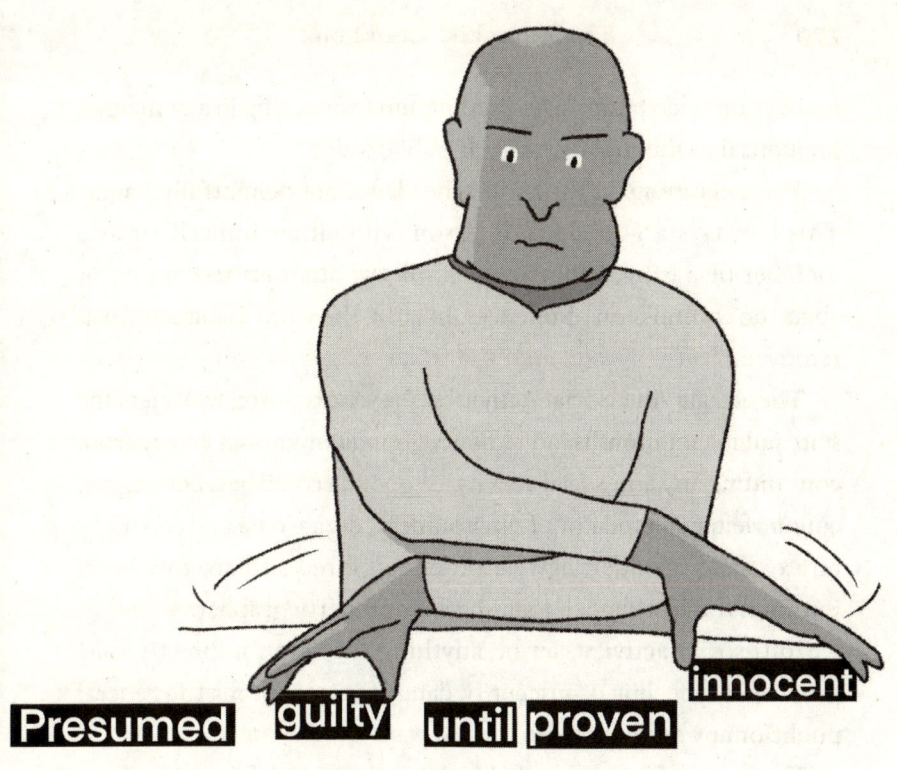

Presumed guilty until proven innocent

Today, Rowlatt Acts have mushroomed in free India, allowing the State to lock up individuals who have committed no crime. There are laws legislated by the Centre as well as individual states. They are written as broadly as possible to allow the State to detain (a fancy term meaning jail) individuals without many, or even any, safeguards.

Their names reveal how sweeping some of these laws are. For instance: The Tamil Nadu Prevention of Dangerous Activities of Bootleggers, Drug-offenders, Forest-offenders, Goondas, Immoral Traffic Offenders, Sand-offenders, Sexual Offenders, Slum-grabbers and Video Pirates Act, 1982.

It allows for detention without charge or trial of up to twelve months of 'any bootlegger or drug offender or forest offender or goonda or immoral traffic offender or sand offender or slum grabber or video pirate ... to prevent him from acting in any manner prejudicial to the maintenance of public order.'

The definitions in this, and other laws, are delightfully vague. This law says a goonda is a person who either himself or as a member of a gang, habitually commits or attempts to commit or abets the commission of offences. In 2014, the word 'habitually' was removed.[140]

The Kerala Anti-Social Activities (Prevention) Act, 2007, lets the state jail for six months 'any known goonda or known rowdy from committing any anti-social activity'. A goonda could be a bootlegger, counterfeiter, depredator of environment, digital data and copyright pirate, drug offender, hawala racketeer, hired ruffian, rowdy, an immoral traffic offender, loan shark or property grabber.

Anti-social activity can be anything that even indirectly may produce 'any feeling of insecurity, danger or fear among the general public or any section thereof'.

Karnataka's Prevention of Dangerous Activities of Acid Attackers, Bootleggers, Depredator of Environment, Digital Offenders, Drug Offenders, Gamblers, Goondas, Immoral Traffic Offenders, Land Grabbers, Money Launderers, Sexual Predators and Video or Audio Pirates Act, 1985, lets the state jail people for twelve months.

The Andhra Pradesh Prevention of Dangerous Activities of Boot-Leggers, Dacoits, Drug-Offenders, Goondas, Immoral Traffic Offenders and Land Grabbers Act, 1986, also allows jailing for twelve months. The state has another law, the Andhra Pradesh Prevention of Dangerous Activities of Communal Offenders Act, 1984, which allows for jailing of up to six months if it is felt the 'public order' could be disturbed.

The Odisha Prevention of Dangerous Activities of Communal Offenders Act, 1993, also can jail people for up to a year to maintain order. The Gujarat Prevention of Anti-Social Activities Act, 1985, the

Jharkhand Control of Crimes Act, 2002, the West Bengal (Prevention of Violent Activities) Act, 1970, and the Rajasthan Prevention of Anti-Social Activities Act, 2006, all allow for a similar jail term.

The Assam Preventive Detention Act, 1980, allows for jailing without charge or trial for two years.

The Himachal Pradesh Preservation of Forest and Maintenance of Supplies of Forest-Based Essential Commodities Act, 1984, allows jail of up to a year. The Jammu and Kashmir Public Safety Act, 1978, should have been repealed with the other laws of the erstwhile state when the Centre gutted Article 370 in 2019, but it has been retained. This is because it allows the State to jail individuals it has demonized as 'stone-pelters' and 'separatists' and 'anti-nationals'.

Other than the regional laws, there are also centrally-legislated laws that allow the State to lock people up without a crime. These are the National Security Act, 1980 (twelve months), Conservation of Foreign Exchange and Prevention of Smuggling Act, 1974 (two years) and the Prevention of Illicit Traffic in Narcotic Drugs and Psychotropic Substances Act, 1988 (two years).

India's preventive detention laws provide for an advisory board to examine whether there is sufficient cause to keep the individuals jailed. These are usually not functional and there is no interest from the State to ensure the rights of those detained. This apathy is endemic and shows also in the rights of those who cannot afford their own legal counsel and are to be provided with legal aid by the State.

Even with more power against the individual than any other modern democratic nation, Indian governments want more. Uttar Pradesh has set up a police force that can arrest without a warrant and without the orders of a magistrate.

This is a power that other states and even the Centre has. We have no civic or popular pushback against this sort of acquisition of power. In the absence of this, the State will continue to acquire more power against us.

As far as the criminal justice system goes, what we practically have in India today is autocracy and tyranny under a democratic name. This is not an accusation against any party because the government is controlled by different political parties at the level of the province. There is no difference, as the laws show, between one part of India and another in this matter.

We may not like the individuals who are being tried by the criminal justice system today because we have made up our minds that they are bad people, even though we have never actually met them.

But we should not approve the State's appropriation of overwhelming power against the individual merely because of dislike. This principle is wrong in law and unjust on the face of it.

21

Rewriting the Law

Democracy is meant to be the rule of the people. But it is also possible that democracy is used to become the rule of the State.

At the beginning of this book, we have referred to the intrusion into the rights of individual citizens by the State and how it undermines your rights and promotes its own. This is the list of laws that shows how this is done legislatively.

When passed and implemented, these laws given below are democratic in essence. But it is obvious that they violate the spirit and fundamentals of democracy. Merely opposing them after they are passed is then portrayed as being undemocratic or 'anti-national'.

How serious are the State's attempts to trample over our rights? To understand, let us have a look at the laws in independent India that are at the core of what we are discussing, many of which are being passed, revived or amended to give the State unprecedented power.

You are a terrorist because I say so

Unlawful Activities (Prevention) Act, 1967

In July 2019, the Modi government amended the anti-terror law UAPA. Named relatively innocuously, the Unlawful Activities (Prevention) Act is a candidate for the most draconian law in the democratic world.

Already harsh before it was amended, the law now gives the State the power to designate, without conviction or trial, any individual as a 'terrorist'. It can do so by determining that the individual is preparing for terrorism or promoting terrorism or even 'is otherwise involved' in terrorism.

There is no anticipatory bail here. The State can then jail them, refuse to share the evidence with those accused for six months and then requires them to prove they are innocent if they must even get bail.

It requires that the 'person charged is able to prove that he has not taken part in the activities of the organization at any time during its inclusion in the Schedule as a terrorist organization'. How does one prove innocence when one doesn't know what the case or evidence is? They can also be deprived of the means of contesting the case legally, with the State authorized to seize their property without conviction.

Bail is denied if there are 'reasonable grounds for believing that the accusations ... are prima facie true'. The State has taken this to mean no bail to be granted at all. Those arrested in the Bhima Koregaon case, where Dalits met to celebrate an event, were jailed despite not being present at the event and not being mentioned in the original complaint. They include lawyers, a poet and an academic, none of whom has a criminal record.

Once notified as a terrorist (in the government gazette), an individual can apply to the government to get off the list. If this application is denied, the individual can seek a review, but there is no time limit set for this review.

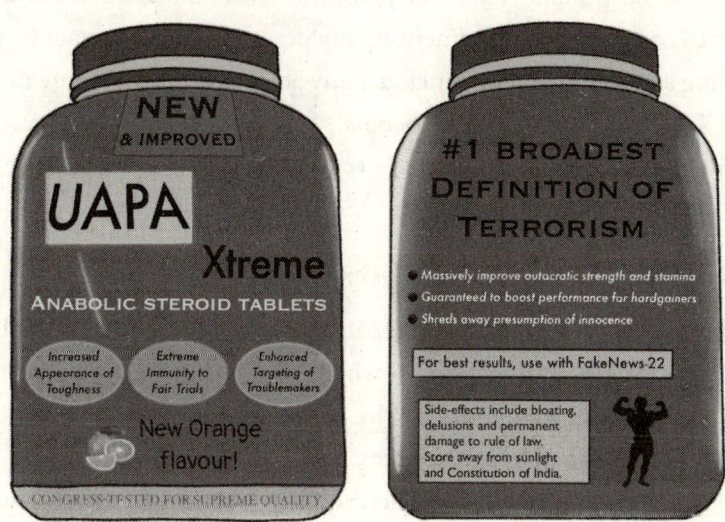

Harsh terror laws are not effective tools. In the 4,349 cases where the now repealed Prevention of Terrorism Act was applied, only thirteen individuals were convicted.[141] POTA replaced the Terrorism and Disruptive Activities (Prevention) Act under which over seventy-six thousand individuals were arrested,[142] with a similar conviction rate, destroying thousands of innocent lives.

Before the amendment, UAPA only allowed organizations to be categorized as 'terrorist'. The State can now categorize any individual as a 'terrorist'. Once the person is so categorized, their name will be added to the list in Schedule 4 of the Act.

These individuals may not even have any affiliation with any of the thirty-six terrorist organizations referred to in the First Schedule of the Act to be classified as terrorists.

Further, the amendment now defines a 'terrorist act' as one that causes 'injuries to any person, damage to any property, an attempt to over awe any public functionary by means of criminal force and any act to compel the government or any person to do or abstain from doing any act etc.'. It also includes any act that is 'likely to threaten' or 'likely to strike terror in people', giving absolute power to the government to brand any citizen or activist a terrorist without these acts being actually committed.

The Gujarat Control of Terrorism and Organised Crime Act, 2015

Approved by the president in 2019, this law was blocked by the UPA under Manmohan Singh when Modi was chief minister of Gujarat. It was written up by the Modi government in Gujarat in 2003 and returned by former president A.P.J. Abdul Kalam, who, in 2004, objected to a section which admitted telephonic interception as evidence.

This continued over the years, with Modi refusing to make the changes and the Centre refusing to let the bill become law.

The law has an overbroad definition for what is organized crime and terrorist acts. It clubs extortion, land grabbing, contract killing, economic offences, cybercrimes, prostitution and demanding ransom with using bombs, dynamite, firearms, lethal weapons, chemicals, poison, and the destruction of public property, disruption of essential supplies.

It also has an open definition of what is organized crime and says that violence or intimidation or coercion 'by an individual, singly or jointly' or as a syndicate constitutes organized crime.

An organized crime syndicate is defined as a group of two or more people.

The law makes a confession before a police officer admissible in court. This provision has been problematic in India because of the conditions under which such confessions are extorted by a police force that has no real accountability.

Then home minister P. Chidambaram opposed this clause. Another one he objected to gives the State extraordinary power over the conditions of bail.

Bail is to be denied if the public prosecutor opposes it. It can only be given if the judge has to be satisfied that the accused is innocent. This means that the burden of proof is reversed. If the accused cannot convince the judge by producing conclusive proof of innocence, he remains in jail. It is not the for the State to produce the evidence of his guilt. Chidambaram said that the court should have the power to grant bail even if the public prosecutor opposes it.

Modi did not want to make the changes and said that the amendments suggested by the Centre amount to taking away the teeth and nails of the Gujarat Control of Organised Crime Act. And also that 'when it comes to dealing with terrorists, we must draw a clear line between those who are on their side and those who are on the side of society.'[143]

When the law was passed again in the state assembly ignoring all the objections, a group of Muslim activists sent a letter to then president Pranab Mukherjee, signed in their blood. The group included the professor J.S. Bandukwala, and its note read: 'Preventive detention laws from MISA to TADA to POTA have been widely misused in Gujarat. Victims have been predominantly Muslims and deprived segments. This happened even during Congress rule. One shudders at what will befall us when the powers at the state and Centre rests with forces that are so alienated from Muslims.'[144]

Arrested for being anti-national

Sedition: Section 124A of the Indian Penal Code
A colonial-era relic, the sedition law was enacted by the British to repress India's independence struggle. Mahatma Gandhi, who was imprisoned under the law, called it 'the prince among the political sections of the Indian Penal Code designed to suppress the liberty of the citizen.'

In 1898, Section 124A of the IPC was amended to include any comment that could be—in any way—construed as an attack upon the government itself, its existence, its essential characteristics, its motives, or its feelings towards people. The colonial government, particularly the Bombay government, followed the changes in the law with a spate of prosecutions against newspapers. In 1908, the British enacted the Newspapers (Incitement to Offences) Act, a law that empowered District Magistrates to confiscate printing presses that published seditious material. They also enacted the Seditious Meetings Act to prevent more than twenty people from assembling for meetings. These measures came in for severe criticism from Bal Gangadhar Tilak.

Courts have ruled that any expression must involve incitement to imminent violence for it to amount to sedition. But the law has been used again and again to arrest journalists, activists and human rights defenders simply for expressing critical views.

The sedition law is excessively vague and broad, making it an easy tool to stifle dissent and debate. There is no good way to apply Section 124A. It does not comply with international human rights laws. It violates the Right to Freedom of Expression under the Indian Constitution. And it goes against India's tradition of tolerance.

Are we a police state?

Armed Forces Special Powers Act (AFSPA), 1958
Section 4 of AFSPA empowers officers (both commissioned and non-commissioned) in a 'disturbed area' to 'fire upon or otherwise use force, even to the causing of death not only in cases of self-defence but against any person contravening laws or orders prohibiting the assembly of five or more persons'.

Suppose an order is passed and assembly of five or more persons is prohibited. Anyone on the scene will be 'acting in contravention of any law or order'. Normally, that person can be arrested. But, in a disturbed area, armed with special powers, the officer may

- fire upon the person even to the causing of death, if he thinks it is necessary;
- destroy any shelter or structure from which armed attacks are likely;
- arrest, without warrant, any person against whom the officer has a reasonable suspicion that he has committed or is about to commit a cognizable offence and may use such force as may be necessary to make the arrest; or
- enter any premises, without warrant, to recover any person, property, arms or ammunition and may use such force as may be necessary.

Section 7 of the Armed Forces (Jammu and Kashmir) Special Powers Act enhances the protection provided to members of the security forces by requiring sanction or permission from the central government before members of the military or other security forces can be prosecuted in civilian courts. In the Army's case, the authority concerned is the Ministry of Defence. For cases involving members of the internal security forces, permission has to be obtained from the Ministry of Home Affairs.

In January 2013, the Supreme Court appointed a commission headed by N. Santosh Hegde, a former Supreme Court judge, in response to a public interest litigation seeking an investigation into 1,528 cases of alleged extrajudicial executions committed in Manipur between 1978 and 2010. The Commission was established to determine whether six cases randomly chosen by the court were 'encounter' deaths—where security forces had fired in self-defence against members of armed groups—or extrajudicial executions. It was also mandated to evaluate the role of the security forces in Manipur.

The Commission, whose report was submitted to the Supreme Court in April 2013, concluded that all the cases it had investigated involved 'fake encounters' (staged extrajudicial executions).[145] It also found that AFSPA was widely abused by security forces in Manipur. Notably, it reported that only one request for sanction to prosecute a member of the Assam Rifles under Section 7 of the Act had been made since 1998.

The Justice Hegde Commission proposed that all cases of 'encounters' resulting in death should be immediately investigated and reviewed every three months by a committee. It also recommended the establishment of a special court to expedite cases of extrajudicial killings within the criminal justice system, and that all future requests for sanction for prosecution from the central government be decided within three months, failing which sanction would be deemed to be granted by default.

'The AFSPA is an obnoxious law that has no place in a modern, civilized country. It purports to incorporate the principle of immunity against prosecution without previous sanction. In reality, it allows the Armed Forces and Central Armed Police Forces to act with impunity', then home minister P. Chidambaram said.

In May 2015, he wrote: 'If there is one action that can bring about a dramatic change of outlook from Jammu and Kashmir to Manipur, it is the repeal of AFSPA, and its replacement by a more humane law.'

AFSPA is unique in many respects. I cannot recall any other law made by Parliament which applies only to the Seven Sisters of the Northeast—Arunachal Pradesh, Assam, Manipur, Meghalaya, Mizoram, Nagaland and Tripura. In 1990, Parliament passed a similar law that would apply to Jammu & Kashmir.

In August 2011, the State Human Rights Commission (SHRC) in Jammu & Kashmir stated that it had found 2,730 unidentified bodies buried in unmarked graves in three districts of north Kashmir.[146] The SHRC announced its intention to attempt to identify the bodies through DNA sampling. Nothing came of it, of course. As we have seen, Kashmiris are treated differently from other Indians in many ways.

Right to Information (Amendment) Act, 2019
This gives the Centre the powers to set the salaries and service conditions of Information Commissioners at central as well as state levels. The original Act set the terms of the central Chief Information Commissioner and Information Commissioners at five years (or until the age of sixty-five, whichever was earlier). The

amendment said that the appointment will now be 'for such term as may be prescribed by the Central Government'. This gave the Centre influence over the individuals it was appointing.

The amendment also gave the Centre authority to arbitrarily fix salaries, allowances and other terms of service of the Chief Information Commissioner and the Information Commissioners. The change says this money 'shall be such as may be prescribed by the Central Government'.

Democracy does not begin and end at the polling station. A real democratic space is transparent. What the government does with our money is not the private business of the government and the money is not the personal property of a minister. We are entitled to know exactly how spending happens. Similarly, the business of running the apparatus of the government concerns all of us. RTI information throws light on who is being given government contracts, at what rate, how many teachers and doctors are employed, how vaccines are distributed, how much politicians pay themselves and what properties they and their relatives own, what the crime rates are and all the things that affect us as citizens and individuals. In that sense, the RTI Act's enactment was a victory for us over the State.[147]

And yet, India is becoming progressively less transparent. The RTI Act has been undermined so much that India has fallen four places in the global RTI rankings since 2013. The reasons that have been cited are blanket exceptions for various security, intelligence, research and economic bodies. The Indian legal framework also does not allow access to information held by private entities which perform a public function.

Uttar Pradesh Recovery of Damage to Public and Private Property Ordinance (2020)
Enacted after the Uttar Pradesh Police shot dead twenty-one protesters and killed two others during the protests against the

Citizenship Amendment Act, this law gives the state government the power to set up tribunals to decide damages to any public or private property due to riots, hartals, bandhs, protests, or public processions.

The tribunal will issue notice for the appearance of the other side. Even if the party does not appear, the tribunal can hear the matter and order attachment of his properties. All orders passed by the tribunals would be final and cannot be appealed before any court.

Temporary Suspension of Telecom Services (Public Emergency or Public Safety) Rules (2017)
This law gives the Union and state governments the power to suspend for any reason mobile and internet services.

Authority is given to the Secretary of the Ministry of Home Affairs in Delhi or the Secretary of state governments in charge of Home Affairs. Failing these two, authority can also be given to any officer of the rank of Joint Secretary or above. The reasons for suspension will be reviewed by a committee within twenty-four hours, but there is no time limit for how long the suspension can last. The law was used in Haryana and Uttar Pradesh during the farmers' protest outside Delhi in 2020-21. In Kashmir, of course, the suspension has lasted for months. Kashmiri students spent all of the 2020-21 lockdown without access to education because they had no internet. Kashmiris could not access tele-medicine during the lockdown for the same reason. This is more than a denial of rights: It is a punishment at the collective level that is unconscionable.

Once the principle of the government having control over our internet is accepted, it is only a question of where this can be applied. It began with Kashmir and came to the farmers but these are only the more famous examples. India leads the world's in internet shutdowns.[148] More shutdowns happen to you as a user than to people in any other nation. And all this in a nation where the Supreme Court says that access to the internet is a Fundamental

Right.¹⁴⁹ It is the principle that must be opposed if we are to reclaim our rights here.

The Information Technology (Intermediary Guidelines and Digital Media Ethics Code) Rules, 2021
This oversight mechanism, created without the passage of an Act, would function for the internet as the Ministry of Information and Broadcasting did for TV regulation. The government gave itself the power to censor and regulate all content on the internet and even on messaging services.

It would require messaging services such as WhatsApp, Signal and Telegram to enable the identification of the creator of a piece of content (for example a cartoon criticizing the prime minister that went viral). This requirement of traceability would break the end-to-end encryption that made these services secure. Also, the originator of a message had no control over who forwarded the content, or how many times it was forwarded, or in which fora. Erotic content exchanged by a couple could land up in a place where it would be seen differently.

The rules say there will be an 'oversight mechanism by the Central government' (censorship) of video content that is published on all web-based platforms. The government can block content and also get platforms to publish apologies. Major platforms took the cue and put out a joint 'self-regulation toolkit' to align content with what the government wanted and, more importantly, not publish or broadcast what it did not want.¹⁵⁰ Presumably, they were encouraged by the fact that the Modi government called their executives in and threatened to jail them.

The Information Technology Act, 2000, did not cover news media. This change was pushed through by adding powers far beyond those in the parent legislation. The rules gave the government the right to regulate content put out by a 'publisher of news and current affairs content'—an open-ended, vague and arbitrary definition. The rules exempt e-newspapers, meaning that established publishing houses (meaning those that receive money from the government through Directorate of Advertising and Visual Publicity [DAVP]) would have an advantage over independent media houses.

This move by the government affects you as a citizen and social media user in three ways. First, it seeks to intrude into your privacy. If you exchange messages with friends or family, and that message is seen by someone who finds it offensive, the government can seek intrusive access to your devices and your life. This eliminates the private and safe spaces we have and subjects everything we do to control.

Second, it brings to heel social media platforms and gives the government a say on what can and cannot be allowed to be said or shown by you. This is not what social media users are subjected to in other democracies.

Third, it puts pressure on independent journalism platforms, which tend to be usually in the digital space, to toe the line of the government. The sweeping and absolute powers the government gives itself in censoring and blocking content means that you will be deprived of information on the conduct of government that those in power do not want you to read.

Industrial Relations Code, 2020
The Lok Sabha cleared this law which introduces more conditions restricting the rights of workers to strike, and more freedom for employers to fire workers.

It requires industrial employees to give a sixty-day notice for a strike. It also forbids strikes during the pendency of labour proceedings before a Tribunal and a further sixty days after the conclusion of such proceedings, making strikes impossible. The law it replaced said employees in a public utility service (water, electricity, natural gas, telephone) could not go on strike unless they gave a six-week notice. The new code would apply for all industrial establishments.

It also relaxed the rules relating to layoffs and retrenchment in industrial establishments having 300 workers, up from 100 workers in the past. Such firms can retrench employees without government permission.

Unions are usually seen in India as the association of only the blue-collar workers of the organized sector. They are discouraged in white-collar work. Few of us who work in the cities in office spaces have ever been part of a workers' union. But collective action is the fundamental principle behind many of the features of the workspace we have today, including the eight-hour workday and the weekend break. These are relatively recent introductions and came only because of worker pressure. A very substantial portion of India's workers are contract employees not directly hired by a company, but sub-contracted to it. They have no capacity to negotiate better terms and this code reduces their options further. Surely, it cannot be the case that reducing the rights of workers is the only way for companies to succeed? But this code assumes that at the outset by restricting and outlawing legitimate action by workers and tips the scales towards industrialists and corporate interests.

Beef with beef

During his 2014 election campaign, Modi made much of what he called the 'pink revolution', meaning the export and sale of meat, especially beef. He promised to put an end to it. In 2015, he made a series of speeches on the issue encouraging BJP states to ban the possession of beef (cow slaughter had already been banned in these states). This began a spate of violence against Muslims and Dalits, triggering what came to be known as the beef lynching, a category of murder that did not exist before 2015.

Maharashtra Animal Preservation (Amendment) Act, 2015
Under this law anyone found in possession of beef would be jailed for up to five years. It also banned the slaughter of bulls, bullocks and calves.

The Haryana Gauvansh Sanrakshan and Gausamvardhan Act, 2015
Possession of beef punishable by up to five years in jail. Sale of cows for slaughter to another state punishable by seven years in jail. Cow slaughter would attract jail of up to ten years. The burden of proof would be on the accused.

The Gujarat Animal Preservation (Amendment) Bill, 2017
This law extended the punishment for cow slaughter from seven years to life. It allows permanent forfeiture of vehicles transporting animals except under prescribed conditions. It also increased the fine from ₹1 lakh to ₹5 lakh. Gujarat Home Minister Pradipsinh Jadeja said the logic was to equate cow slaughter with murder. The burden of proof in the law was reversed. In 2019, a man was convicted after being accused of using beef in a biryani served at his daughter's wedding. He was asked to prove that the meat, consumed weeks earlier, was not beef. When he was unable to do so he was sentenced to ten years in jail. An embarrassed high court gave him bail and suspended his sentence using the judge's 'judicial discretion'.

In the name of love

Anti-miscegenation laws are those that try to restrict women from marrying whom they want. After 2014, the BJP has pushed a conspiracy theory called 'love jihad' in the public while denying it exists in Parliament.[151] The fiction being spread was that Muslim men were luring Hindu women into marrying them for the purpose of conversion. Why a man would want to do this was not explained or thought about. Merely accusing Muslims was sufficient. Thus began a spate of laws aimed at restricting the rights of women and harassing the families of those they married into, especially if they were Muslim.

Uttarakhand Freedom of Religion Act, 2018
A clause in this law says that 'any marriage which was done for the sole purpose of conversion by the man of one religion with the woman of another religion either by converting himself before or after marriage or by converting the woman before or after marriage may be declared null and void.'

Any relative of the person changing their faith can file a complaint with the police.

The law says that 'if any person comes back to his ancestral religion, then this shall not be deemed conversion', without defining what 'ancestral religion' means.

The District Magistrate will then conduct an inquiry through the police 'with regard to real intention, purpose and cause of that proposed religion conversion'.

The burden of proof to show that the conversion was not fraudulent, through undue influence, coercion, or by marriage, is on the person being converted. If the State feels there was facilitation in the conversion, then the burden of proof is also reversed on that individual, meaning the husband, wife and the family, or the priest.

Those who change their faith without applying to the government 'in the prescribed proforma' and without the consent of the government after the police inquiry face a year in jail.

Himachal Pradesh Freedom of Religion Act, 2019
Chief Minister Jairam Thakur, who is from the BJP, said that in the past thirteen years, 'not even a single case was filed under the 2006 Act', referring to an anti-conversion law passed by the Congress

government.[152] He said this lack of cases necessitated a stronger act against religious freedom.

On 31 August 2012, the High Court had struck down that part of the 2006 law which required a person looking to change their faith to give thirty days' notice to the government. That was brought back by Thakur in this law. Along with this, thirty days' notice was also to be given by the priest officiating the ceremony (if any). After this, the District Magistrate would hold an inquiry to see if the change of faith can be allowed. If the government determines that these conditions have not been met, the conversion is 'illegal and void'. Individuals who change their faith without permission face a year in jail. The punishment for propagation (a Fundamental Right under Article 25) was up to seven years in jail.

Uttar Pradesh Vidhi Viruddh Dharma Samparivartan Pratishedh Adhyadesh, 2020 (Prohibition of Unlawful Conversion of Religion Ordinance)
Popularly known as the 'love jihad' law—though this was copied from laws already existing in other BJP states—prohibits conversion except with government permission and sixty days' notice. Conversions for marriage are illegal. The burden of proof is on the family the woman is marrying into. The punishment is up to five years in jail. FIRs can be filed by any blood relative or relative by marriage or adoption against anyone for unlawful conversion of either person in the marriage.

Madhya Pradesh Dharma Swatantreya Adhyadesh, 2020 (Freedom of Religion Ordinance)
It replaces the Religious Freedom Act of 1968. The law punishes conversion through marriage with ten years in jail. It also nullifies such marriages. Children born in these nullified marriages could

claim the right to their father's property. Conversions can only happen with government permission and sixty days' notice. FIRs can be filed by parents and siblings of either person in the marriage. Any other person who is related by blood, marriage, adoption, guardianship or custodianship can file a written complaint with court permission.

Gujarat Freedom of Religion (Amendment) Act, 2021
Similar to the other BJP laws on 'love jihad', the Gujarat law allows any relative by birth or marriage to register a complaint accusing an individual of having coerced their partner to converting for marriage. Punishment is up to five years in jail and a fine of not less than ₹2 lakh. If the 'victim' of conversion was a tribal person or a minor, jail time would be up to seven years and the fine ₹3 lakh. Organizations that were propagating religion would be fined ₹5 lakh and their head jailed for ten years.

The law declares as void marriages 'done for the purpose of unlawful conversion', and says that this will be done by a family court or any other court. The burden of proof is reversed and anyone accused of converting someone under this law is guilty until they prove their innocence.

Without showing any data, the government claimed that it was required to curb the 'emerging trend in which women are lured to marriage for the purpose of religious conversion'.

Piloting the amendment Bill in the House, Gujarat Home Minister Jadeja said 'the amendment was required to stop people from luring Hindu girls into marriage with the intention of religious conversion', and added, without evidence, that 'there is international finance being channelized to lure Hindu girls into marriage and then their conversion'.[153]

The Muslim Women (Protection) of Rights on Marriage Act, 2019
This law criminalizes the utterance of the word talaq three times in one sitting. The divorce emanating from this utterance had already been held illegal by an earlier Supreme Court judgment. In essence, it criminalized the saying of this word together three times by Muslim men even though the marriage remained intact. The law did not change the Muslim personal law of divorce, and the utterance of talaq in three different sittings (separated by menstrual periods and no intercourse) remained valid. The law also takes away the magistrate's discretion for giving bail in case of arrest, requiring the judge to first listen to the view of the wife before freeing the husband. The punishment for saying the word talaq for Muslim men was three years in jail, the same as IPC 154 (rioting with a deadly weapon). Muslim men are the only section of India for whom divorce, a private wrong for all other communities, is a crime against the State.

Who are you and why are you here?

The Aadhaar and Other Laws (Amendment) Act, 2019
The Modi government revived the commercial use of Aadhaar, struck down as unconstitutional by the Supreme Court in

September 2018. The law reopened the door for exploitation by private entities and businesses built on data aggregation. It allowed authentication by private firms and continued the confusion over voluntary and mandatory. The use of Aadhaar for authentication or offline verification on a voluntary basis is only specified in the new subsections being added to the Aadhaar Act. The specific provisions amending the Indian Telegraph Act, 1885 (which applies to telecom companies) and the Prevention of Money Laundering Act, 2002 (which applies to banks) do not make Aadhaar voluntary. Instead, they say that the relevant entity 'shall identify' clients (meaning fulfil the Know Your Customer process) using Aadhaar, passports or other any other form of identification notified by the Central government.

The option of a passport was really a false choice, since only 5 per cent of Indians have passports. This means Aadhaar will effectively be the only acceptable form of identification for large sections of the population when they try to get mobile numbers or open bank accounts, which would violate the Supreme Court's judgement.

Provisions of the law were amended to allow a service provider to use Aadhaar to verify the identity of an individual, but do not provide a mechanism for the individual to assert receipt of a service. This can be used against individuals who cannot identify themselves, while individuals have no protection against their identity being misused when service is delivered in their name to someone else.

The Citizenship (Amendment) Act, 2019
Muslim refugees from Afghanistan, Bangladesh and Pakistan were excluded from this law, which gave automatic citizenship to non-Muslims (Hindus, Christians, Parsis, Jains, Sikhs and Buddhists) who came to India before 31 December 2014. There were existing routes that could have delivered this; a new law was not needed.

The law did not address the two largest communities of refugees in south India (Tamils from Sri Lanka) and north India (Tibetans). The law assumed that the only persecution in South Asia happens in Muslim states and against non-Muslim individuals. It did not address the groups persecuted for their political beliefs (such as in Myanmar and China) or their sexuality. It did not address those Muslims who were religiously persecuted, such as the Ahmadis and Shias of Pakistan. After the law was passed in late 2019, it was still not implemented in 2021. The framing of its rules was delayed, after severe condemnation from foreign nations and institutions and the widespread protests in India.

The Gujarat Prohibition of Transfer of Immovable Property and Provision for Protection of Tenants from Eviction from Premises in Disturbed Areas Act, 2019 Amendment

A law that kept Muslims segregated and ghettoized was tightened in 2019. The law—known as *Ashant Dharo* (Disturbed Areas Act)—required people to reveal their religion while selling and purchasing property. In areas declared 'disturbed', Hindus could not sell to Muslims and vice versa without government permission. Over the years, and especially after Modi became chief minister, more and more neighbourhoods in all major Gujarat cities have been included under the Act, even those where there has never been rioting. This has effectively ghettoized Muslims.

The Amendment that was cleared in 2019 gave a collector the authority to determine if the sale of a property would lead to the likelihood of 'polarization' or 'improper clustering' of people from a particular religion. It also gave the government power to review the decision of the collector, even if the buyer and seller made no appeal.

Property sales could trigger the creation of a special investigation team with the collector, municipal commissioner and police commissioner as members. The amendment enables the state government to form a committee to advise it on the adding of new areas to the Disturbed Areas Act.

The Amendment enlarged the scope of property transfer and included leasing. In effect, even foreigners can rent and buy property in those parts of Gujarat's cities where Indian Muslims cannot.

Forcible ghettoizing of communities is a violation of our Constitution and Article 19(e) which gives all Indians the right 'to reside and settle in any part of the territory of India'. By allowing laws like the Disturbed Areas Act, we allow the violation of our constitution. This law was meant to be in place temporarily to ensure that people were not displaced during riots. But it has been made permanent and is renewed every five years with no resistance.

Transgender Persons (Protection of Rights) Act, 2019
The law requires India's transgender individuals to submit to a certification process under a section called 'Recognition of identity of transgender persons'. Instead of the right to self-identify and the freedom to determine their sexuality, they have to make an application to the District Magistrate for a certificate of identity. Those who undergo surgery to change their gender must submit a certificate from a medical officer.

A transperson would require this certificate of identity to access a variety of social-welfare programmes that exist or might be offered, including those relating to food, healthcare, educational opportunities and insurance.

Activists had other problems with the law:[154]

That sexual assault on transpeople attracted a maximum term of two years in jail, against a minimum of seven years for women.

If young transpeople wanted to leave home because of pressure to conform to the sex they were born with, they could no longer join the trans community. They would instead have to go to a court, which would send them to a 'rehabilitation centre'.

The law ignored a key demand of the community—that they be given public sector reservation in the way that people with disabilities had been given.

The 2019 law came after an earlier bill, the Transgender Persons (Protection of Rights) Bill, 2016—which, too, was opposed. It defined the transgender individual as a 'person who is neither wholly female nor wholly male'.

It included the proposal for 'screening committees' to determine who was transgender and who was not. It also criminalized begging, a source of income for a large number of transgender Indians.

Foreign Contribution (Regulation) Act, 2010
The FCRA is a strange piece of legislation. It prevents the receipt of foreign money 'for any activities detrimental to the national interest'.

It first appeared in India in 1976 as a law to prevent external interference in the country's electoral process and democracy. It prohibited political parties and their candidates, journalists and newspaper publishers, judges, bureaucrats and members of Parliament from receiving foreign money.

In time, liberalization meant that many of these categories received foreign money legally. For instance, the media, print, television and certainly online—the most dominant form—can not only receive foreign investment, but can be dominated by it. The largest media companies in India are Facebook and Google, which are entirely foreign-owned and managed. Newspapers can receive equity investments from foreign firms, as can news channels.

Even the political parties managed to get themselves off the hook on FCRA. In January 2013, a public interest litigation was filed in Delhi High Court claiming that the Bharatiya Janata Party and the

Congress had received donations from the same company, Vedanta / Sterlite, which were in violation of the FCRA Act. On 28 March 2014, the court held that the BJP and Congress were guilty of violating FCRA and asked the Modi government and the election commission to act against the two parties. The government made amendments in 2018 that let both parties off.[155,156]

Instead, the NGOs were left in the net for the State to regulate their funding. The State decides whether or not an NGO can receive money, how it will spend it and whether it can continue to receive it in future.[157]

While the State has always been hostile to NGOs, through the Modi era, it has been trying actively to cut the size of the NGO sector. India has over thirty lakh such organizations, which range from neighbourhood associations to the most powerful NGO in the world, the Rashtriya Swayamsevak Sangh. NGOs work on education, disaster relief, violence against women, public health, human rights, the criminal justice system, the environment, agriculture and so on. Between 2014 and 2018, a report estimated, there had been about a 40 per cent cut in foreign funding for these groups.[158]

Today, the Indian State welcomes and invites foreign investment in arms and ammunition and bombs and guns, in alcohol and tobacco, petroleum and pharmaceuticals and everything else that one can think of. But it restricts and squeezes investment in India on health, education and rights. Something is very wrong with such a state of affairs.

How does this affect you? In several ways. First, NGOs are the third largest workforce in the US. The retail and manufacturing sectors employ more people than the NGO sector there. In twenty-four American states out of fifty, NGOs actually employ more workers than all the branches of manufacturing combined. It is similar in the UK. In Europe, 13 per cent of all jobs are in the

NGO sector, and this is 2.8 crore jobs in total. To put this figure in perspective, consider that less than 10 per cent of all jobs in India are in the formal sector. Attacking NGOs attacks employment.

Second, NGOs work in spaces where the government is often weak, especially with what is called last-mile delivery—meaning, reaching the people who matter. Small NGOs working on education, health, nutrition, gender, trafficking and other issues are able to effectively do things that the government often cannot because it lacks the capacity. Discouraging or actively attacking them hits their work.

Third, NGOs can help at a time when there is no other source. FCRA stopped Indian NGOs from accessing oxygen and other medical equipment during the second wave of Covid-19 in 2021. The inflexible rules and desire to curb their work meant the NGOs were not able to help out Indians who were dying in thousands because of lack of basic health assistance which could have been made available but was prevented by the law.[159]

Growing concern

Juvenile Justice (Care and Protection of Children) Act, 2015
The idea that children accused of rape should be tried as adults came in the wake of the Nirbhaya incident in Delhi, an accused in which was a minor. This produced a strong sentiment of vengeance in the media which seeped into the polity. On coming to power, the BJP government brought a change in the law which says that if accused of 'heinous offences'—those where the maximum punishment is seven years or more under the Indian Penal Code—children over sixteen should be tried as adults.

The process requires a Board to 'conduct a preliminary assessment with regard to his mental and physical capacity to commit such offence, ability to understand the consequences of the offence and the circumstances in which he allegedly committed the offence'. To divine this, it can take the assistance of 'experienced psychologists or psycho-social workers or other experts'.

The Board itself consists of a judge and two 'social workers' (defined as anyone 'actively involved in health, education, or welfare activities pertaining to children for at least seven years or a practicing professional with a degree in child psychology, psychiatry, sociology or law').

If this Board determines that the child should face trial as an adult, the case is sent to a children's court, which will try the child as an adult, 'considering the special needs of the child, the tenets of fair trial and maintaining a child-friendly atmosphere'. Convicted minors are to be sent to 'a place of safety' till they reach the age of twenty-one, at which point they are sent to an adult jail.

All democracies have imperfect laws. All democracies have laws that restrict the rights of individuals. But they also all accept that over time, the needle of freedom must constantly shift towards the individual and the right of the State to restrict and curb the freedom must reduce.

That is why constitutions such as India's begin with high-minded language extolling liberty and freedom. India's laws have moved in the other direction. They have imposed excessive restrictions and often outright bans on even fundamental rights. And they have given overwhelming power to the State to control and restrict the actions of individuals. This is an aberration in liberal democracies and we must push back against the State and its laws and reclaim the freedoms that the constitution promised us when it was promulgated in 1950.

WHERE 'DEVELOPMENT' EQUALS LAND GRAB

All the laws in this chapter are egregious but most of them sit within the criminal justice system. This one is in a less conspicuous place: the Ministry of Coal.[160]

The Coal Bearing Areas (Acquisition and Development) Act, 1957 is triggered when the government is satisfied of the presence of coal in an area (most often this is in the Adivasi belt). The government then publishes its 'intention to acquire' the property in the government gazette.

- There is no requirement to consult those who own and work on the land
- Those affected who submit written objections within thirty days may get compensation. But they are not entitled to it and there is no requirement for the government to pay anything
- After thirty days, the Centre issues a declaration acquiring the land and all right over it 'shall vest absolutely in the Central government (free from all encumbrances)'
- These rights are transferred to a company such as Coal India Ltd, and may further be given to private companies
- The law has no provision for ensuring that human rights impact assessments are conducted prior to land acquisition proceedings
- There are no requirements to consult non-landowners who may be affected by the acquisition, such as landless labourers.
- The law also does not offer any meaningful protection to communities from forced evictions by the companies
- Communities in the areas have no security of tenure, which the rest of us do when we possess property

Mining for anything other than coal is regulated under the Right to Fair Compensation and Transparency in Land Acquisition, Rehabilitation and Resettlement Act. It requires that 'the consent of 70 per cent of affected families is mandatory where land is sought to be acquired for public-private partnership projects, and 80 per cent for private projects.'

This law also contains a provision requiring the consent of the villages concerned. It requires a social impact assessment—meaning a study by independent experts to map a project's impact on people's lands and livelihoods, and its economic, social and cultural consequences—in consultation with affected communities. This law does not apply to coal-bearing areas.

Several laws that appear to protect Adivasis and others affected by the Coal Act do not actually do anything to prevent violation of rights by the State.

The Scheduled Tribes and Other Traditional Forest Dwellers (Recognition of Forest Rights) Act, 2006, recognizes customary rights over land and other resources.

Members of these communities can claim individual rights over forest land they depend on or have made cultivable. Communities can also file for rights over common property resources, including community or village forests, religious and cultural sites and water bodies.

The law says that village assemblies must have a key role in deciding who has the rights to forest resources. And yet, the Ministry of Tribal Affairs has itself observed that this law is mostly ignored by the government.[161]

Another law regulating land acquisition is the Panchayats (Extension to the Scheduled Areas) Act, also called PESA. It requires that panchayats be consulted before land is acquired in tribal areas for development projects, and also before the resettlement or rehabilitation of people affected by such projects. This law is also more or less ignored.

Then there is the Environment (Protection) Act, which requires all projects of a certain size to get environmental clearance after public consultation with local communities that are likely to be affected. This, again, does not happen. The draft Environment Assessment Impact, 2020, proposed by the Modi government, reduces not just the rights but also the information affected communities can receive.

The one law that the government properly follows and applies is the one under which it grabs land: the Coal Bearing Areas (Acquisition and Development) Act, 1957.

We must also consider what happens to the communities once their lands are acquired and they are evicted. Schools in mining areas are shut between 3 p.m. and 4 p.m. because of explosions so big that the school buildings tremble.[162]

Power companies that use coal are not obliged to dispose of the waste material produced by burning coal. The residue is dumped in something called an ash pond. It sounds innocuous. It is not. The author visited the village of Raigarh in Chhattisgarh and saw some of these ponds. They resemble Mordor. The mounds of black ash are so dense that they become compact and cover—absolutely, without an inch of relief—all the ground as far as the eye can see.

Leave alone vegetation, which has no chance of growing under or around this poison, even the earth is not visible. Another ash pond in the making was an immense area that had been dug so deep that the earth movers cutting into the land seemed to be bugs when seen from a precipice.

This is the finale to the drama that begins with the government publishing the gazette triggering its thirty-day notice. Observing the policies of Coal India Ltd (which controls some two-thirds of all mining in India), a Parliamentary committee in 2007 said tribal communities 'hardly have any access to the official gazette wherein they could see that their lands are to be acquired for public purposes'. But no change has been made to the process of seizing Adivasi property.

This is quite deliberate. The industrial development of this country is happening on the back of our theft of Adivasi land. And we, in the upper class, are complicit.

A good test to know whether this is fair or appropriate is to ask yourself this: Have you ever read (or seen) a government gazette or know where it is published? If the government were to publish something today in its gazette, would you know?

In 2006, the late singer Lata Mangeshkar announced she would leave Mumbai if a flyover was built in front of her mansion on Mumbai's Peddar Road. She said the construction involved would affect her throat. Later, she said that 'if there is drilling on the road, the foundations of many buildings will be shaken', That flyover was, of course, not built.

Which one of us would give up our flats for development? Our elites can even veto the construction of a greatly needed flyover. We insist that others, who are unwilling but weak, make all the sacrifices on our behalf and then we are puzzled when there is violence against the state. Knowing the reality of this naked land grab brings a very different meaning to words like 'Maoist', 'Naxalite' and, of course, 'development'.

SECTION V

Understand Your Privilege and Use It for Change

22

Why India Needs Us to Protest

Some years ago, I spoke at Bengaluru's Mallya Aditi International School, the city's most elite educational institution. My audience was a few hundred of its senior students, aged perhaps sixteen and above. Some parents were also present as, of course, were some teachers.

I spoke about privilege, which is something that even I, approaching fifty at that time, had begun to understand only recently.

India is said to be a nation of extremes. Where the world's most expensive residence—the Antilia skyscraper which houses four members of the Ambani family—is in the same city as Asia's largest slum. Rich and poor exist side by side in our cities, as we know. What is referred to as middle class in India is actually the upper class by the definition of the rest of the world. Only 5 per cent of Indians have passports. A substantial portion of these are held by those who work as labourers in the Gulf nations. It is the so-called middle class that holds the other 2 or 3 per cent, travelling abroad for holidays or education. If you are part of this set, as I am, we are the elite.

I once worked closely in Mumbai with a man visiting from Australia. We would sometimes go for lunch from our newspaper office in Parel to a restaurant in Worli, a drive of about fifteen or twenty minutes. This required us to stop at a few traffic lights, where we would encounter hawkers selling books and newspapers, and beggars, including children. Of course, being Indian and having lived with this all my life, I was oblivious to what was on the street next to me and had become inured to it. My Australian colleague was not. One day, a little girl, perhaps eight or so, tapped on the car's window and made a gesture of eating. He asked me: 'What is her future?'

I was embarrassed by the question and thought of saying something defensive: her family can work but chooses to beg instead; or something along those lines as comes naturally to people like me when confronted with difficult and uncomfortable questions about our privilege. I chose instead to tell the truth as I saw it: 'She has no future.'

The rich are getting richer and the poor getting poorer

There was no chance this girl would lead a meaningful life. She would receive little or no education. She was unlikely to ever get a decent, salaried job. She would not know economic, emotional or physical security as I had known it. She was and would continue to be exposed to assault, violence and brutality—including by the State. She would be constantly anxious about things—the next meal, the next place to sleep, the next bath, the next predator. This was not a future, if a future meant the prospect of success or happiness.

And here was the most absurd part of this: There were many more Indians like her than there are like you and me.

The poverty line is ₹47 a day for urban India and ₹32 a day for rural India.[163] Meaning that if you made ₹1,407 per month in a city and ₹972 elsewhere, you are not considered poor. The number of Indians surviving on less than this sum is thirty-five crore—the combined populations of the UK, France, Italy, Spain and Germany. The number of Indians making just this much or a little more is perhaps twice this number.

The World Bank's global poverty line is ₹142 per day, which comes to ₹4,275 per month. By this standard, India perhaps has 100 crore poor people.

The average farm household in India earns ₹6,400 per month. If this is a family of five people, individual income would just be around ₹1,280 a month. Such a family would not be considered poor. But it would be unable to eat at a restaurant, pay the fees at a private school, send children to college, or go on vacation. The bulk of its money would be spent on food and daily expenses.

The term 'daily-wage worker' is often used without being fully understood: These are people who do not eat if they do not work. And there are crores of Indians in this category.

What is it like to live on these numbers that define the poverty line? In 2011, *The New York Times* reported the story of two twenty-six-year-old men, an investment banker from Singapore and a computer science graduate from Massachusetts Institute of Technology (MIT), who tried living on ₹100 each per day in Bengaluru.

Tushar Vashisht and Mathew Cherian had returned to India to join the Aadhaar project. They had calculated the sum using the average per capita income in India (based on GDP) of ₹4,500 a month.

From this, they took out a third to rent a 10' x 6' room, leaving them with ₹3,000 each for the month to spend on food, transport, communications, utilities and the rest.

Remember that ₹100 is twice the urban poverty line and three times the rural one.

The two men spent three weeks on ₹100 per day. The paper reported that one of them lost four kilograms and the other two kilograms in this period. They went through bouts of dizziness and even depression from a lack of nourishment. They could rarely afford milk. They could not afford toiletries.

Their lives were geographically limited. All the things a family living on such a sum needed to access—the place of work, school, shops—needed to be within a five kilometre radius.

At the end of three weeks, the two were left with savings of ₹350. If they faced an economic shock, say an accident, they had no means to overcome the difficulties produced by the loss of income. Of course, the two men did not actually do the sort of work that India's poor do—hard physical labour exposing them to higher levels of danger than engineers and bankers.

For their final week, they decided to cut their daily expenses to ₹32, the poverty line for rural India. This sum was the spending limit India's Planning Commission had arrived at in a controversial affidavit it had filed with the Supreme Court to define the poor. Those who spent at least ₹32 a day on food, education and health care would not be counted as poor and would therefore be ineligible for government subsidies, the affidavit had said.

The two men decided to go to Kerala, spending the ₹350 they saved on two train tickets. For a week, they lived in a 12' x 12' room lent to them by a friend in Karukachal, a town near Kottayam. They would now have to cook over a wood fire, drink well water and wash their clothes outside.

After deducting what the Planning Commission estimated the poor paid for rent, utilities and transport, they would have ₹17 a day for food, about one-third what they had spent in Bengaluru in their first three weeks. The other ₹8 they could use for non-food expenses including the use of mobile phones. They only accepted incoming calls or gave people missed calls so that they could call them back. They learned that a labourer needed three thousand calories a day but could not afford the food required to get those. Proteins would help but they could not afford them, not even eggs. So the diet almost entirely comprised carbohydrates: wheat, rice and bananas. 'For a manual labourer working close to three thousand calories a day, purely burning through carbohydrates in the day without proteins means that his muscle structures won't develop, leading to an early onset of arthritis and other illnesses', Vashisht was quoted as saying in a BBC report.

What they found in their brief one-month experiment is borne out by data that the government itself provides. A report from around the same period said the caloric intake of Indians in rural areas had drastically fallen over thirty years. While India's economy had been growing at 6 per cent each year, the poor had been making less than before after inflation and could no longer afford to eat what they could earlier.

The nutritional requirement that was recommended was a national norm of 2,400 kilocalories a day for rural areas and 2,100 calories a day for urban areas, the difference being attributed to the lower rate of physical activity in urban areas.

But rural calorie consumption per day had fallen from 2,221 calories in 1983 to 2,047 calories in 2004-05, a decline of 8 per cent.

The urban calorie consumption fell 3.3 per cent from 2,080 calories in 1983 to 2,020 calories in 2004-05.[164] Punjab was the best performing state in India, and Madhya Pradesh the worst. The rural protein consumption fell 8 per cent. In three decades, there had been no rise in non-cereal (rice and wheat) consumption.

And, mind you, the numbers represented an average. In rural areas, 81 per cent of Indians did not consume the recommended levels. In urban India, the figure was 57 per cent. The calorie consumption for the poorest Indians was significantly lower than the top quartile despite the poor requiring more calories because of the manual work they did.

A survey conducted by the government between July 2017 and June 2018 showed that things had deteriorated: The average amount spent by Indians in a month had fallen in 2018 compared to 2012. Adjusted for inflation, the average fell from ₹1,501 to ₹1,446. In 2012, it had risen 13 per cent over two years.[165]

This report said there had never been a time in the last fifty years that consumption had decreased, and that such a collapse indicated an increase in poverty in the country by at least 10 per cent. The most worrying trend in the report was a dip in food consumption. The amount spent on food by urban Indians remained flat—₹946 per person per month in 2018 compared to ₹943 in 2012. But rural Indians were spending less on food in 2018 (₹580) compared to 2012 (₹643).

How the poor live and what that has done to their bodies

The International Food Policy Research Institute's Global Hunger Index in 2021 showed that India had fallen forty-six places globally from fifty-five to 101.[166] The index measured hunger, stunting in children and undernourishment. India's fall put it behind Pakistan, Bangladesh and Nepal with the prevalence of child wasting (low weight for height) in 2014–19 increasing to 17.3 per cent from 15.1 per cent in 2010–14.

The numbers have been consistent. During 2000–07, too, nearly half of India's children under the age of five years were malnourished. This was the worst in South Asia and worse than the worst performer in the African region. Government data said that the absolute weight and height of Indians, on an average, had not shown any improvement over the last quarter century.

India's rank on the Human Development Index of the United Nations did not change between 2014 and 2020 though India claimed to be the world's fastest growing economy for parts of this period.

The National Family Health Survey of 2019-20[167] revealed that states recorded a significant fall in four key metrics, which represent the nutritional status of children, in 2019-20 compared to 2015-16. In states like Gujarat, Maharashtra and West Bengal, the share of anaemic and wasted (low weight for height) children was significantly higher than the levels recorded in 2005-06. This indicated a reversal of progress that had been hard to win. Even in states such as Kerala, which continued to lead in these indicators, the levels recorded in 2019-20 were poorer than the 2015-16 figures.

The survey, which put out data for twenty-two states and union territories, also analysed ten major states.

This analysis found that anaemia among children was higher in all ten states in 2019-20 compared to 2015-16. In Gujarat, Himachal Pradash, Maharashtra and West Bengal, a higher percentage of children were anaemic in 2019-20 than in 2005-06.

The percentage of wasted children was also higher in half of the ten states. In Assam, Gujarat, Karnataka, Maharashtra and West Bengal, a higher percentage of children were wasted in 2019-20 compared to 2005-06.

In seven of the ten states analysed, a higher percentage of children were underweight (low weight for age) in 2019-20 compared to 2015-16.

Stunting (low height for age) was higher in six out of the ten states compared to 2015-16.

The study also found that incidents of diarrhoea had increased in half the states including Andhra Pradesh, Bihar, Gujarat, Maharashtra, Karnataka and West Bengal. In Bihar, it was up from 10.4 per cent in 2015-16 to 13.7 per cent in 2019-20.

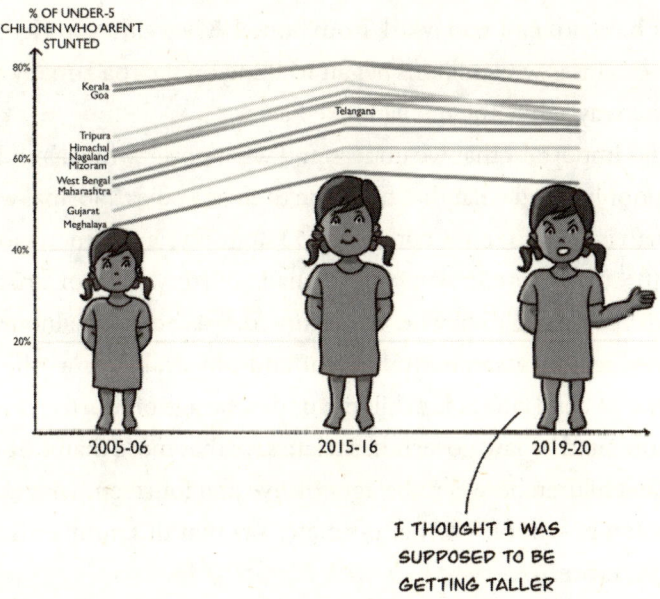

More than twenty-two crore Indians sought work under the Mahatma Gandhi National Rural Employment Guarantee Act (MGNREGA), 2005, in 2020.

MGNREGA pays a daily wage of ₹200 but can only offer work to households for no more than 100 days a year. Meaning one household can only get 100 days or fewer in a year—work can be shared between different adult members of the household—and about a third of the Indians who ask for this work do not get it. The registration process involves applying to the Gram Panchayat which then issues job cards. Work is to be provided fifteen days after this. But Panchayat Samitis may not meet for months, resulting in sanctioning of work getting delayed.[168] Only 10 per cent of 4.8 crore households managed to fully benefit with 100 days of work in 2015-16. Twenty-three crore Indians, more than the population of the UK, fell into poverty in 2020.[169] This was the price of the lockdown, an event many of us celebrated with the banging of utensils. The poor have no option to 'work from home'. They either work or they starve. This is why millions began walking on the road, many dying on the way, while the media looked away.

It is important that we understand what poverty means and how the poor live and what that has done to their bodies. Normal weight at birth is 3.5 kilograms and even 4.5 kilograms is common globally. In 2015, two crore Indian children had a birth weight of under 2.5 kilograms.[170] Children who were stunted, wasted and malnourished cannot lead the same intellectual and physical lives as the rest. Although child labour for children under the age of fourteen in India is prohibited by law, government data says that more than 1.01 crore Indian children between the ages of five and fourteen work instead of going to school.[171] Other estimates say that this number is more like six crore.

And this will not surprise us—evidence of it is available to those who just go to the street and look around. India's children add to the livelihood of their families by working in fields, factories, mines, in shops, residences and in sex work.

One in four Indian children has no access to education.[172] They will never be able to get a salaried job that gives them a decent wage.

Crores of Indian girls are married off before they are eighteen.[173] Crores of them become mothers when they should be studying or building a career. Many of them die at childbirth. Toys are something the majority of Indian children will not own or experience.

The perspective that many of us have for those Indians who are marginalized (a word that means the treatment of a person or community as peripheral and insignificant) is not fully understood or appreciated. India is a strange place where a group of people who are discriminated against by society and the State are still accused of being appeased.

The serious problem of exclusion

A government report by former justice Rajinder Sachar released in late 2006 revealed some of the data on India's Muslims. It said that across India, banks had identified a number of Muslim concentration areas as 'negative geographical zones' where bank credit and other facilities are not easily provided. Muslims received only a third of the advances they should have, including priority sector advances.

Half of all of India's villages where Muslims were 40 per cent or more of the population were less likely to have access to a road. Such places were also less likely to have educational institutions, medical facilities, post and telegraph offices or a bus stop.[174] Where there is a concentration of Muslims, the Indian State is more likely to become delinquent and reduce its delivery.

Muslim children in north India were the only ones to have no access to pre-school unless they give up their mother tongue, there being no anganwadis with Urdu instruction. Article 29 gives all Indians 'having a distinct language, script or culture of its own ... the right to conserve the same'. But often, Urdu schools had teachers who had no knowledge of Urdu, as we have noted earlier. The problem was compounded by the fact that these posts were reserved for Scheduled Caste and Scheduled Tribes and such candidates were not available. Muslims from the Scheduled Castes have no access to SC reservation.

This was another serious problem of Muslim exclusion, the Committee revealed. The first Backward Classes Commission submitted its report in 1955. It identified 2,399 castes and communities as being backward. Of these 837 were considered the 'most backward' and deserving of special focus and attention. This list contained Hindu as well as Muslim groups. However, as the Sachar report says, this 'did not find approval from the chairperson of the Commission and one of the reasons cited was the assumed castelessness of Muslims and Christians'.

The denial of SC benefits to Muslims goes back to 1936, when the Imperial (Scheduled Caste) Order was passed. The order, which denied SC status to Christians and Buddhists, included Muslim groups in the SC list, because they were clearly identifiable. But they were barred from availing benefits, making their inclusion meaningless. This imperial decree was the basis on which independent India has continued to deny Muslims inclusion in the SC category, though it chose to include Buddhists later. As many as twenty lakh Muslims, who identify as SC or ST, have been denied benefits due to this decision.

This view that Muslims and Christians do not need reservation because they are casteless is commonly held but is incorrect in two ways. For one thing, even caste among Hindus is not sanctified by the Constitution which forbids Hindu practices such as untouchability. If its existence in one part of society is taken for granted, it must be assumed to be present elsewhere. In that sense, caste is a social and cultural phenomenon and not a legal one. For another, the documentation of disadvantaged and marginalized Muslim caste groups is thorough and undisputable.

The Sachar report said that the Constitutional (Scheduled Caste) Order of 1950 gives the status of SC only to Hindu groups having 'unclean occupations', while the Dalit Muslims have been classified with the Other Backward Classes. Thus, Dalit Muslims and OBC Muslims are in the same reservation category. Dalit Muslims cannot access SC reservation in employment and education.

The 1950 order has been amended twice to include, first, Dalit Sikhs in 1956 and Dalit Buddhists in 1990, leaving only Dalit Muslims and Dalit Christians out of the SC list.[175] Puzzlingly, Sikhs and Buddhists are notified as religious minorities by the National Commission for Minorities along with Muslims and Christians (and Parsis and Jains). So, clearly, it is not just their official status as religious minorities that is behind India's denial of rights to Dalit Christians and Dalit Muslims.

The Sachar report refers to Uttar Pradesh's Banjara tribal community whose Hindu members are included in the ST list but not its Muslim members. The Mandal Commission clubbed arzal and ajlaf together in an all-encompassing OBC category, 'overlooking the disparity in the nature of the deprivations they faced'. According to the Sachar report, 'being at the bottom of the social hierarchy, the arzals are the worst off and need to be handled separately. It would be most appropriate if they were absorbed in the SC list.'

The problem of Muslim exclusion extended to OBC Muslims as well. One obstacle here was that Muslims were often not issued the requisite OBC caste certificates by officials.

The Sachar committee also looked at the data on employment of Muslims in government and found that their representation compared to their share of population was about a third of what it should be and preponderantly in the lower ranks. Muslims made up only 4.9 per cent of the total eighty-eight lakh state and central government employees, according to data submitted by various departments.

The Railways had 4.5 per cent Muslims while state banks and the Reserve Bank of India had 2.2 per cent. The share of Muslim employment in central public sector units was 3.3 per cent. It was better in state PSUs at 10.8 per cent.

This, however, does not reveal the whole picture. In the Railways, 98.7 per cent of the Muslims employed were at lower levels, with only 1.3 per cent as Group A or Group B officers. SC and ST composition in contrast was 18 per cent in this set.

Government employment was desirable for two reasons. First, because the government remains the largest employer of the organized sector in India. Of all organized sector jobs in 2004, 70 per cent were in government and only 30 per cent in the private corporate sector. And, therefore, it is crucial that Muslims and other marginalized groups find representation here.

Second, government employment gave individuals a privileged position through 'ascribed and sometimes assumed status', as a result of which they were accorded status and protocol privileges as representatives of the government. In a pluralistic society, the report added, reasonable representation was necessary to enhance participatory governance.

Among the elite bureaucrats—belonging to the Indian Administrative Service, the Indian Police Service and the Indian Foreign Service—Muslim representation was 3.2 per cent. Here, the committee accepted that the share of Muslims appearing for the examination was also low (4.9 per cent) and that their success rate in clearing the exam appeared to be on a par with the rest. In the judiciary, Muslims made up 7.8 per cent, compared to 23 per cent OBCs and 20 per cent SC/STs.

In the security agencies, India's Muslims face open discrimination. They are assumed to be treasonous by birth and for this reason, not hired. Earlier in this book, we have touched on the reluctance of India's intelligence agencies to hire Muslims. The country's the entire intelligence community comprising R&AW, IB, National Technical Research Organisation and Military Intelligence, had a single Muslim officer.

In the security forces, the Sachar report secured data on five lakh of the nineteen lakh people employed. Of the people employed in Border Security Force, Central Industrial Security Force, Sashastra Seema Bal and Central Reserve Police Force, the representation of Muslims was 3.6 per cent in the higher categories and 4.6 per cent in the lower. Almost all Muslims (96 per cent of the total) were in the lower levels, with only 2 per cent of them making it to Group A or Group B officer levels. The data from the military was not made available to the Sachar committee for whatever reason. In 1999, however, former defence minister Mulayam Singh Yadav revealed that of the over ten lakh people in the Indian military, Muslims comprised only 1 per cent.

The observations made here are important because they could have led to action. Article 16(4) of the Constitution gives the State the authority to make 'any provision for the reservation of appointments or posts in favour of any backward class of citizens which, in the opinion of the State, is not adequately represented in the services under the State'.

On this subject, the Venkatachaliah Committee had told the Vajpayee government: 'An effort needs to be made to carry out special recruitment of persons belonging to the under-represented minority communities in the police forces of states, paramilitary forces and armed forces.'

Nothing was done on this by that government or the ones that followed.

The India Justice Report 2019 released by the Tata Trusts[176] said that between 1999 and 2013, Muslim representation in the Indian police has remained consistently low, at between 3 per cent and 4 per cent outside Jammu and Kashmir. The inclusion of the erstwhile state pushes the national figure up to 8 per cent. This means there are more Muslim policemen for the around one crore people of Jammu and Kashmir than there are in the rest of India's 135 crore population.

Excluded and discriminated against by the State and facing discrimination from large parts of society, Muslims have the highest proportion of self-employed people in India (39.4 per cent), more than Hindus as a whole (29.6 per cent) and SCs/STs (22.9 per cent). Muslim women (29.1 per cent) were twice as likely to be self-employed in a household enterprise than Hindu women (14.9 per cent). Informal sector employment in Muslims in urban areas was 92.1 per cent compared to 76.9 per cent for Hindus.

The Sachar report says, 'Muslims, especially women, have virtually no access to government development schemes. They experience discrimination in getting loans from the Jawahar Rozgar Yojana for below poverty line beneficiaries, in getting loans for housing, in procuring widow pensions.'

The report also said that while it was not easy to identify all the causes for the marginalization of Muslims in these schemes, one was the 'lack of Muslim participation in the political process and governance, especially at the local level'. The enhancement of this in electoral politics by parties and policymaking by government was important.

Despite being burdened by disadvantages, on many social issues, Muslims are ahead of Hindus. Their sex ratio of 986 is much higher than the national average (Gujarat's is only 890). Their infant and under-five mortality rates are better than the national average.

And yet, Muslims are casually stigmatized in India. Many of us repeating the demonstrably false chant that India's Muslims are being 'appeased'. This is a slander that is inflicted on them by the few. Kashmir's children spent the entire year of 2020 without internet or school but we are angered at the fact that they protest against India's behaviour with them. We call them separatists and jihadis and stone-pelters, and having coined these words we can hate them more easily and accept what is being done to them in their homes and their own state. Laws that allow the State to lock up Kashmiris—including minors—for up to two years without a trial become acceptable once we have pigeonholed these individuals and branded them. Blinding them with birdshot, arbitrarily discharged by men from other states, is approved. Tying up a Kashmiri to the bonnet of an official vehicle and parading him through villages as a 'lesson' and a 'message' to other Kashmiris is not a crime but an act that is recognized and felicitated.

India, one of the world's most unequal societies, is unequal also in this way. One set of Indians determine what is nationalistic, right, and acceptable and what is punishable, wrong and unacceptable. This is based not on the law or the constitution, but on our prejudices.

> **LACK OF MUSLIM REPRESENTATION IN POLITICS**
>
> In 2002, the Justice Venkatachaliah report, referring to Muslim political representation, had told the Atal Bihari Vajpayee government: 'Backward classes belonging to religious minorities who have been identified and included in the list of backward classes and who, in fact, constitute the bulk of the population of religious minorities should be taken up with special care along with their Hindu counterparts in the developmental efforts for the backward classes.'
>
> This was ignored. Today, there is no Muslim among the ruling party's 303 Lok Sabha MPs. There was no Muslim among its 282 Lok Sabha MPs between 2014 and 2019 as well. There is no Muslim chief minister in India. In fifteen states, there is no Muslim minister at all. In ten states, there is one Muslim minister, usually given the minority affairs portfolio. In Uttar Pradesh, even the minority affairs ministry which manages waqf properties is run by a non-Muslim.

Lack of representation of some harms all

It is the Indian 'middle class' which deals in such narratives. It is tiny but has forced its opinion on the many.

The British middle class is 60 per cent of the population. The working class, the set of people employed in labour and other blue-collar work, is 14 per cent. In India, what is called the middle class is so small that it is statistically just a blip. Statisticians sometimes speak of a plus/minus 2 per cent error in numbers. Such an error would wipe out the entire Indian 'middle class'. And yet, it is the most dominant and visible set of our population. It is this set that controls the media which is locked into it because it survives on advertising.

What you and I consume pays the media. So it is not surprising that the media's content is focused on us, the 3 per cent, and not the many.

Dalits (twenty crore), Adivasis (ten crore) and Muslims (19.5 crore) make up nearly 40 per cent of India's population. How much representation do they have in our economy, our political power structure and in our media?

An Oxfam study in India, conducted between October 2018 and March 2019,[177] found that 106 of 121 newsroom leadership positions were occupied by the upper castes.

Three out of every four anchors (among a total of forty anchors in Hindi channels and forty-seven in English channels) of debates are upper caste. Not one was Dalit, Adivasi or OBC. News channels drew the majority of the panelists from the upper castes, for over 70 per cent of their primetime debate shows.

No more than 5 per cent of all articles in English newspapers are written by Dalits and Adivasis. Only ten of the 972 articles featuring on the cover pages of the twelve magazines under the study were about issues related to caste.

The idea that their rightful places are 'stolen' by the Dalit and the Adivasi and that reservations are the undoing of 'merit' is universally accepted by India's elite. Stories with headlines such as 'Over 60 per cent OBC, SC positions vacant in IIMs' clearly debunk this belief. More than 90 per cent of the posts of professor reserved for Adivasis in universities were not filled. Of over 6,000 vacancies in forty-two universities, 75 per cent were those that dealt with reserved categories. Even our institutions of learning where reservation was legally mandated were uncomfortable with Dalit and Adivasi faculty. They need the rest of us to show solidarity with them.

* * *

This, then, was the issue I touched upon very briefly in my talk at that elite Bengaluru school. The idea that we were privileged and that it was incumbent upon us to recognize that and to act towards it. If we meant to be good Indians and good patriots, the most important contribution we could make was our own participation in its improvement. We could set aside some of our privilege and give it to those who did not have it. Our Constitution tells us India is a society of equality, liberty and fraternity but it cannot be the responsibility of the government or of political parties to hold these values. They must be held by us, the citizenry. We could cede some of our space to those less fortunate purely because of an accident of birth and willingly give them reservation.

This did not go down well. The students were hostile to the idea. They felt they had earned their position in life, and their place in the school through their merit. If others had not, this was not their concern. Even the parents were angered by the idea of reservation.

There was unanimity among the audience—and I would call it a consensus—that reservation was bad and that they, the individuals in this school, were unconnected to any notion of privilege.

I was disappointed, of course, but not surprised. This is who we are as a society. The school could not be expected to be very different from the society which had produced it. Would the audience, and the children in it, especially, have continued to hold their views if they had been better acquainted with the reality of India and with the data? I do not think so. We are all humans and fraternity is at the heart of humanity. If they had known how things really were, they would have a different opinion of other Indians, one arising out of empathy. But a talk is not a book and it is not possible to communicate something of the magnitude of what was being attempted to be communicated in a thirty-minute lecture. My intervention was not meaningful: I left the children and their parents knowing nothing more than what they had already known.

It is because we have become inured to poverty, deprivation and marginalization that we can continue to ignore it while still assuming that India will rise to become a great power. The reality is that the vast majority of its population alive today will die in poverty or destitution. Change will come to India—it comes to all societies in time. But we can quicken it. Crores will continue to suffer in a nation whose defence spending is four times that of health. Whose arms and weapons spending is five times that of education. The budget that is allocated and spent on food for the poor has reduced in recent times because hunger has increased, according to the data produced by the world and by the Indian government itself. We celebrate the arrival of ₹59,000 crore warplanes which we cannot even use in combat because the very nature of war has changed.

This prioritization is the result of the stranglehold that the upper class, us, has on the polity in India. So, it is incumbent on us to try and change it.

The most effective way to change our world is by investing time in learning and finding out about the world we live in and communicating and spreading that knowledge to others.

WHY INDIA NEEDS US TO PROTEST

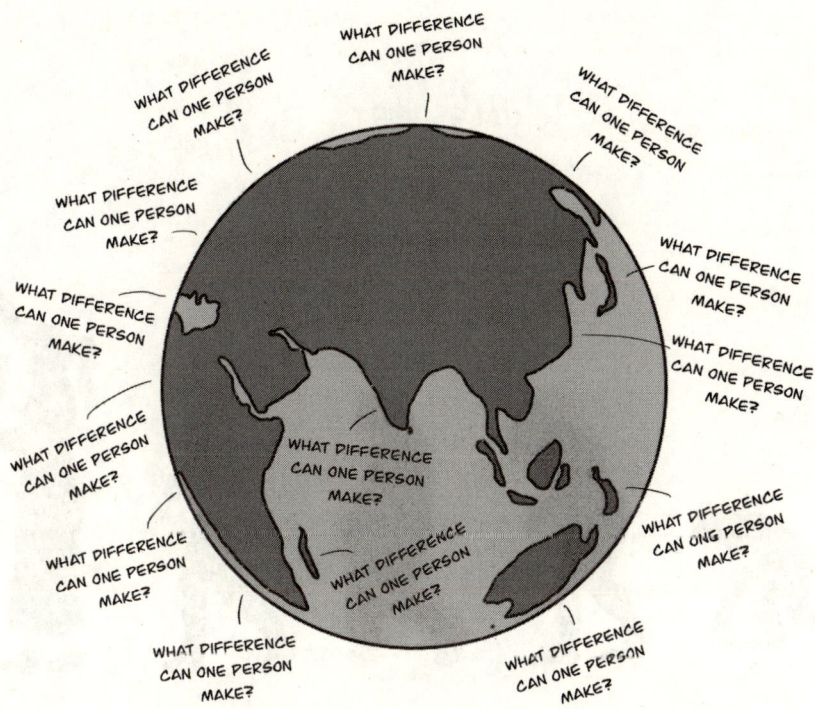

Notes

1. Praveen Chakravarty, 'Why So Few Indians Pay Income Tax?', BQ Prime, 28 September 2020, https://www.bloombergquint.com/opinion/why-so-few-indians-pay-income-tax
2. N.A. George and F.H. McKay, 'The Public Distribution System and Food Security in India', *PubMed Central*, Volume 16, Number 17 (2019), https://www.ncbi.nlm.nih.gov/pmc/articles/PMC6747310/
3. 'The State of Food Security and Nutrition in the World', Food and Agriculture Organization of the United Nations, 2021, https://www.fao.org/publications/sofi/2021/en/
4. 'Railway Registers Worst Punctuality in 3 Years, 30% Trains Ran Late in 2017-18', *Hindustan Times*, 4 May 2018, https://www.hindustantimes.com/india-news/railway-registers-worst-punctuality-in-3-years-30-trains-ran-late-in-2017-18/story-BXrvwTgyg44Mcj990JaCCK.html
5. Yuthika Bhargava, 'Railways to Restart Passenger Services in Phased Manner', *The Hindu*, 11 May 2020, https://www.thehindu.

com/news/national/coronavirus-lockdown-railways-to-resume-select-passenger-train-services-from-may-12/article31551514.ecc
6. Ritika Khera, 'Impact of Aadhar in Welfare Programmes, SSRN, 2 October 2017, https://papers.ssrn.com/sol3/papers.cfm?abstract_id=3045235
7. Syed Zafar Mahmood, 'Summarised Sachar Report on Status of Indian Muslims', *The Milli Gazette*, 13 December 2006, https://www.milligazette.com/dailyupdate/2006/200612141_Sachar_Report_Status_Indian_Muslims.htm
8. 'Chhattisgarh Govt Allows Inter-state Public Transport Operations', *Business Standard*, 27 August 2020, https://www.business-standard.com/article/current-affairs/chhattisgarh-govt-allows-inter-state-public-transport-operations-120082700839_1.html
9. '102 Airports Post ₹1,646.66 Crore Loss in FY18-19: Govt Data', *BusinessLine*, 22 March 2020, https://www.thehindubusinessline.com/economy/logistics/nearly-75-per-cent-of-airports-owned-and-managed-by-aai-made-losses-in-fy-2018-2019/article31134783.ece
10. Vakasha Sachdev, 'Even Without the NRC, Here's Why the CAA Is Unconstitutional', The Quint, 24 January 2020, https://www.thequint.com/videos/news-videos/why-caa-is-unconstitutional-article-14-counters-to-government-arguments-supporting
11. Prakash Louis, 'Dalit Christians: Betrayed by State and Church', ResearchGate, Volume 42, Number 16 (April 2007), https://www.researchgate.net/publication/262127045_Dalit_Christians_Betrayed_by_State_and_Church
12. Saikat Datta, 'Muslims and Sikhs Need Not Apply', Outlook, 5 February 2022, https://www.outlookindia.com/magazine/story/muslims-and-sikhs-need-not-apply/233087

13. Akshaya Nath, 'Tamil Nadu: "Untouchability wall" Around Dalit Colonies Triggers Protest', India Today, 28 July 2021, https://www.indiatoday.in/india/story/tamil-nadu-untouchability-wall-around-dalit-colonies-triggers-protest-1833862-2021-07-28
14. Sukanya Roy, '30 Years of SC/ST PoA Act: Lacks and Loopholes', TwoCircles.net, 6 November 2020, https://twocircles.net/2020nov06/439780.html
15. Aakar Patel, 'UAPA (Amendment) Bill 2019 Violates the Very International Law It Quotes, Defies Principles of Natural Justice', Firstpost, 3 August 2019, https://www.firstpost.com/india/uapa-amendment-bill-2019-violates-the-very-international-laws-it-quotes-defies-principles-of-natural-justice-7104391.html
16. Rakshit Sharma, 'Cow Slaughter in India', IJLPP, https://ijlpp.com/cow-slaughter-in-india/https://ijlpp.com/cow-slaughter-in-india/
17. Jayanth K. Krishnan, 'India's Patriot Act: POTA and the Impact on Civil Liberties in the World's Largest Democracy', *Minnesota Journal of Law & Inequality*, Volume 22, Issue 2, https://scholarship.law.umn.edu/cgi/viewcontent.cgi?article=1058&context=lawineq; Bhadra Sinha, 'Confession in Police Custody Weak Evidence: SC', *The Hindustan Times*, 5 February 2011, https://www.hindustantimes.com/delhi/confession-in-police-custody-weak-evidence-sc/story-41uq7vJpRyHKEqdDKaRwvL.html
18. A. Vaidyanathan, 'Threat To Human Rights "Highest In Police Stations": Chief Justice Ramana', NDTV, https://www.ndtv.com/india-news/threat-to-human-rights-highest-in-police-stations-chief-justice-ramana-2505776;
19. Umang Poddar, 'In India, Five People Die in Official Custody Every Day. How Does the Law Deal With These?', Scroll.in, 14 November 2021, https://amp.scroll.in/article/1010500/in-india-five-people-die-in-police-custody-every-day-how-does-the-law-deal-with-these-deaths

20. 'India: Annual Report on Torture 2019', Uncat.org, 26 June 2020, http://www.uncat.org/wp-content/uploads/2020/06/INDIATORTURE2019.pdf
21. 'India: Annual Report on Torture 2019', Uncat.org, 26 June 2020, http://www.uncat.org/wp-content/uploads/2020/06/INDIATORTURE2019.pdf
22. Full list here: Aakar Patel, '"Rowlatt Acts" India Gifted Itself', *Business Standard*, 15 February 2019, https://www.business-standard.com/article/opinion/rowlatt-acts-india-gifted-itself-119021401451_1.html.

    The acts are Gujarat Prevention of Anti-Social Activities Act of 1984; Uttar Pradesh National Security Act; Tamil Nadu Prevention of Dangerous Activities of Bootleggers, Drug-offenders, Forest offenders, Goondas, Immoral Traffic Offenders, Sand-offenders, Sexual Offenders, Slum-grabbers and Video Pirates Act, 1982; Karnataka Prevention of Dangerous Activities of Acid Attackers, Bootleggers, Depredator of Environment, Digital Offenders, Drug Offenders, Gamblers, Goondas, Immoral Traffic Offenders, Land Grabbers, Money Launderers, Sexual Predators and Video or Audio Pirates Act, 1985; Assam Preventive Detention Act, 1980; Bihar Conservation of Foreign Exchange and Prevention of Smuggling Act, 1984; Jammu & Kashmir Public Safety Act; West Bengal Prevention of Violent Activities Act of 1970.
23. The Statesman, https://www.thestatesman.com/not-found/constitutionality-of-anti-conversion-laws-44674.html
24. Aakar Patel, 'Keep the Faith (or Else)', in *Our Hindu Rashtra* (India: Westland, 2020).
25. 'Haryana Becomes 11th State to Table "Love Jihad" Law, Congress Protests in Assembly', The Wire, 5 March 2022, https://m.thewire.in/article/communalism/haryana-becomes-11th-state-to-table-love-jihad-law-congress-protests-in-assembly/amp

26. Mohamed Imranullah S., 'State Entitled to Administer Temples Despite Being Secular', *The Hindu*, 18 September 2020, https://www.thehindu.com/news/national/tamil-nadu/state-entitled-to-administer-temples-despite-being-secular/article32634795.ece; L. Ravichander, 'To Uphold Secularism, Free Temples from State Control', *Deccan Chronicle*, 23 April 2021, https://www.deccanchronicle.com/opinion/columnists/220421/l-ravichander-to-uphold-secularism-free-temples-from-state-control.html
27. Aakar Patel, 'Punishing Crimes That Didn't Happen', in *Our Hindu Rashtra* (India: Westland, 2020).
28. Faizan Mustafa, 'When It Comes to Violation of Religion, Can the State Be Held Monetarily Liable?', The Wire, 4 September 2017, https://thewire.in/law/comes-violation-freedom-religion-can-state-held-monetarily-liable
29. Shaju Philip, 'After Historic SC Anthem Win, Kerela Siblings Went to School for a Day', *The Indian Express,* 4 December 2016, https://indianexpress.com/article/india/jehovahs-witnesses-sect-after-historic-sc-national-anthem-win-kerala-siblings-emmanuel-went-to-school-for-a-day-4409478/
30. *Sachar Committee Report*, p. 18: https://www.minorityaffairs.gov.in/sites/default/files/sachar_comm.pdfhttps://www.minorityaffairs.gov.in/sites/default/files/sachar_comm.pdf
31. 'Supreme Court Urged to Relook Order on Posting of Teachers in Minority-Run Institutions', *The Hindu*, 31 January 2020, https://www.thehindu.com/news/national/supreme-court-urged-to-relook-order-on-posting-of-teachers-in-minority-run-institutions/article30706043.ece
32. Apoorva Mandhani, '99% Habeas Corpus Pleas Filed in J&K Since Article 370 Move Are Pending, HC Bar Tells CJI', The Print, 28 June 2020, https://theprint.in/judiciary/99-habeas-corpus-pleas-filed-in-jk-since-article-370-move-are-pending-hc-bar-tells-cji/450281/

33. The Economist Intelligence Unit, 'Democracy Index 2020: In sickness and in health?', https://www.eiu.com/n/campaigns/democracy-index-2020/.
34. Reporters Without Borders, https://rsf.org/en/ranking
35. Freedom House, 'Freedom in the World 2021', https://freedomhouse.org/country/india/freedom-world/2021
36. Betwa Sharma, 'India Suffers "Alarming" Decline in Civil Liberties, Kashmir Ranked "Not Free": 2020 Freedom Report', Huffpost, 4 March 2020, https://www.huffpost.com/archive/in/entry/india-human-rights-kashmir-2020-freedom-report_in_5e5f35edc5b67ed38b3a553e
37. Freedom House, https://freedomhouse.org/country/india/freedom-world/2021
38. 'WJP Rule of Law Index 2020', World Justice Project, https://worldjusticeproject.org/our-work/research-and-data/wjp-rule-law-index-2020
39. Aakar Patel, *Price of the Modi Years* (India: Westland Non-Fiction, 14 November 2021).
40. https://monitor.civicus.org/country/india/
41. https://monitor.civicus.org/Ratings/
42. Rashmi Rajput, CBI Carries Out Raid at Teesta Setalvad's Premises Alleging Embezzlement', *The Indian Express,* 14 July 2015, https://indianexpress.com/article/india/india-others/cbi-carries-out-raid-at-civil-rights-activist-teesta-setalvads-premises/
43. 'Office Premises of NGO Raided; Indira Jaising Named in FIR', *BusinessLine,* 11 July 2019, https://www.thehindubusinessline.com/news/cbi-searches-at-residence-of-indira-jaising-offices-of-lawyers-collective/article28380723.ece
44. Karan Manral, 'ED Attaches Properties Worth Rs 17.66 Crore of Amnesty International India', *Hindustan Times,* 16 February 2021, https://www.hindustantimes.com/india-news/

ed-attaches-properties-worth-rs-17-66-cr-of-amnesty-india-others-101613483933122.html

45. Arvind Ojha, 'Raid at Greenpeace Office, ED Claims Evidence of Corruption', *India Today*, 11 October 2018, https://www.indiatoday.in/india/story/raid-at-greenpeace-office-ed-claims-evidence-of-corruption-1360468-2018-10-11

46. Syed Khalique Ahmed, 'FCRA Licence Cancelled, NGO Navsarjan Lays Off All Staffers', *The Indian Express*, 27 December 2016, https://indianexpress.com/article/cities/ahmedabad/fcra-licence-cancelled-ngo-navsarjan-lays-off-all-staffers-4440969/

47. 'India: Rights Groups Harassed Over Foreign Funding', Human Rights Watch, 26 June 2019, https://www.hrw.org/news/2019/06/26/india-rights-groups-harassed-over-foreign-funding

48. Deeptiman Tiwary, 'FCRA Licences of 6,600 NGOs Cancelled in Past Three Years: Govt to Lok Sabha', *The Indian Express*, 18 March 2020, https://indianexpress.com/article/india/fcra-licences-of-6600-ngos-cancelled-in-past-three-years-govt-to-lok-sabha-6319507/

49. 'India: Democracy Threatened by Growing Attacks on Civil Society', Civicus, 9 November 2017, https://www.civicus.org/index.php/media-resources/reports-publications/2991-india-democracy-threatened-by-growing-attacks-on-civil-society

50. Aloke Tikku, 'Home Ministry Cancels Registration of 9,000 Foreign-Funded NGOs', *Hindustan Times*, 28 April 2015, https://www.hindustantimes.com/india/home-ministry-cancels-registration-of-9-000-foreign-funded-ngos/story-UpnVtwpwSrSJzqEdYygiJN.html

51. 'Govt Banned 14,500 NGOs under FCRA Act from Receiving Foreign Funds', *Business Standard*, 4 December 2019, https://www.business-standard.com/article/pti-stories/14-500-ngos-banned-by-govt-from-receiving-foreign-funds-119120400877_1.html

52. Omar Rashid, 'Allahabad HC Sets Aside NSA Order Against Kafeel Khan, Asks UP to Release Him Forthwith', *The Hindu*, 1 September 2020, https://www.thehindu.com/news/national/other-states/allahabad-hc-sets-aside-nsa-against-kafeel-khan-asks-up-to-release-him-forthwith/article32493509.ece
53. Niha Masih and Joanna Slater, 'Evidence Found on a Second Indian activist's Computer Was Planted, Report Says', *The Washington Post*, 6 July 2021, https://www.washingtonpost.com/world/2021/07/06/bhima-koregaon-case-india/; Jignesh Mevani and Meena Kandasamy, 'There Is No Case. Release the Bhima Koregaon 16 and Compensate Them', The Wire, 22 April 2021, https://thewire.in/rights/bhima-koregaon-arrests-activists-arsenal-report
54. Aarefa Johari et al., 'From Pune to Paris: How a Police Investigation Turned a Dalit Meeting Into a Maoist Plot', Scroll.in, 2 September 2018, https://scroll.in/article/892850/from-pune-to-paris-how-a-police-investigation-turned-a-dalit-meeting-into-a-maoist-plot
55. Malavika Murali, 'Almost Rs 1,700 Crore Spent on Advertisements in Three Years: Centre', *Hindustan Times*, 8 December 2021, https://www.hindustantimes.com/india-news/almost-rs-1700-crores-spent-on-advertisements-in-3-years-centre-101638936017747.html
56. Vasudha Venugopal, 'I&B Ministry Had Cited Security Report to Reject Raghav Bahl's Application', *The Economic Times*, 12 October 2018, https://economictimes.indiatimes.com/industry/media/entertainment/media/ib-ministry-had-cited-security-report-to-reject-raghav-bahls-application-for-tv-channel/articleshow/66173189.cms?from=mdr
57. Pratap Bhanu Mehta, 'Whichever Way the Sudarshan TV Case Turns Out, Dark Days Lie Ahead', *The Indian Express*, 19 September 2020, https://indianexpress.com/article/opinion/columns/sudarshan-tv-case-hate-speech-propaganda-6601740/

58. Shubhra Gupta, 'When Deepika Padukone Visited JNU, It Was Loudest Bollywood Had Spoken Out on Issues', *The Indian Express*, 12 January 2020, https://indianexpress.com/article/india/jnu-violence-attack-deepika-padukone-aishe-ghosh-chhapaak-6211979/
59. 'Wife Suggested Moving Out of India: Aamir on Intolerance', *The Hindu*, 28 November 2021, https://www.thehindu.com/news/national/aamir-khan-on-intolerance-in-india/article7909340.ece
60. Tarique Anwar, 'Delhi Riots: Cops Name Eminent Academics and Activists in Chargesheet, But Say They're Not Accused', News Click, 13 September 2020, https://www.newsclick.in/delhi-riots-cops-name-eminent-academics-and-activists-chargesheet-say-theyre-not-accused
61. Sindhu Hariharan, 'How Many Tweets Did Twitter Remove As Requested by Indian Govt in H2 2019?', *Times of India*, 21 August 2020, https://timesofindia.indiatimes.com/business/india-business/how-many-tweets-did-twitter-remove-as-requested-by-indian-govt-in-h2-2019/articleshow/77667430.cms
62. Kumar Sambhav Shrivastava, '40 Government Departments Are Using a Social Media Surveillance Tool – and Little Is Known of It', Scroll.in, 4 September 2018, https://scroll.in/article/893015/40-government-departments-are-using-a-social-media-surveillance-tool-and-little-is-known-of-it
63. 'Government Officials Skip House Panel Meet on Pegasus', *The Hindu*, 28 July 2021, https://www.thehindu.com/news/national/parliamentary-panel-not-allowed-to-discuss-pegasus/article35588921.ece
64. https://monitor.civicus.org/Ratings/
65. 'Indian Kashmir: Freedom in the World 2020', Freedom House, https://freedomhouse.org/country/indian-kashmir/freedom-world/2020.

66. Amitabh Behar, 'Behind the New Rules for NGOs to Get Foreign Funds, a Clear Political Message – Fall in Line', Scroll.in, 24 September 2020, https://scroll.in/article/973909/behind-the-new-rules-for-ngos-to-get-foreign-funds-a-clear-political-message-fall-in-line
67. 'Losing Sight in Kashmir: The Impact of Pellet-Firing Shotguns', Amnesty International, 13 September 2017, https://www.amnestyusa.org/reports/losing-sight-in-kashmir-the-impact-of-pellet-firing-shotguns/
68. 'Update of the Situation of Human Rights in Indian-Administered Kashmir and Pakistan-Administered Kashmir from May 2018 to April 2019', UNHR, 8 July 2019, https://www.ohchr.org/Documents/Countries/PK/KashmirUpdateReport_8July2019.pdf
69. 'Update of the Situation of Human Rights in Indian-Administered Kashmir and Pakistan-Administered Kashmir from May 2018 to April 2019', UNHR, 8 July 2019, https://www.ohchr.org/Documents/Countries/PK/KashmirUpdateReport_8July2019.pdf
70. 'Urging the Republic of India to End the Restrictions on Communications and Mass Detentions in Jammu and Kashmir As Swiftly As Possible and Preserve Religious Freedom for All Residents', Congress.gov, 6 December 2019, https://www.congress.gov/bill/116th-congress/house-resolution/745/text
71. 'Apply Mind Before Using Pellet Guns: Supreme Court', *Hindustan Times*, 14 December 2016, https://www.hindustantimes.com/india-news/apply-mind-before-using-pellet-guns-supreme-court/story-hRMYWkwNPS0aeUFlbN4p8O.html
72. 'Apply Mind Before Using Pellet Guns: Supreme Court', *Hindustan Times*, 14 December 2016, https://www.hindustantimes.com/india-news/apply-mind-before-using-pellet-guns-supreme-court/story-hRMYWkwNPS0aeUFlbN4p8O.html
73. 'Supreme Court Directs J&K HC to Decide in 6 Weeks on Plea Seeking Ban on Use of Pellet Guns', News 18, 22 July 2019,

https://www.news18.com/news/india/supreme-court-directs-jk-hc-to-decide-in-6-weeks-on-plea-seeking-ban-on-use-of-pellet-guns-2241317.html

74. Shuja-ul-Haq, 'Use of Pellet Guns Can't Be Prohibited in J&K, Says High Court', *India Today*, 11 March 2020, https://www.indiatoday.in/india/story/use-of-pellet-guns-can-t-be-prohibited-in-j-k-says-high-court-1654483-2020-03-11

75. 'Parle, Bajaj Refuse to Air Their Ads on "Toxic" News Channels: Swara Bhasker, Konkona Sen Sharma Laud Brands', *Hindustan Times*, 13 October 2020, https://www.hindustantimes.com/bollywood/parle-bajaj-refuse-to-air-their-ads-on-toxic-news-channels-swara-bhasker-konkona-sen-sharma-laud-brands/story-7YspNpQzMZoSBDbhi30CNP.html

76. Kritika, 'OpIndia Loses Ads After UK-Based "Stop Funding Hate" Campaign', The Quint, 29 May 2020, https://www.thequint.com/news/webqoof/opindia-loses-ads-after-uk-based-stop-funding-hate-campaign

77. Imran Qureshi, 'FIR Registered Against Aakar Patel, Former Director of Amnesty International India Over a Twitter Post', BBC News, 5 June 2020, https://www.bbc.com/hindi/india-52933793

78. 'FIR Against Aakar Patel for Tweets on Ghanchi Community', *The Indian Express*, 4 July 2020, https://indianexpress.com/article/india/surat-fir-against-journalist-aakar-patel-over-objectionable-tweets-6488274/

79. '6,221 Pellet-Gun Injuries Reported in Unrest after Burhan killing: J&K govt', *Times Of India*, 24 January 2018, https://timesofindia.indiatimes.com/india/6221-pellet-gun-injuries-reported-in-unrest-after-burhan-killing-jk-govt/articleshow/62641050.cms

80. Oxford University Press, 2016.

81. New Internationalist Publications Ltd, 2011.

82. Billy Perrigo, '"Non-Lethal" Weapons in Kashmir', *Time*, 6 September 2018, https://time.com/longform/pellet-gun-victims-kashmir/

83. Routledge, 2010.
84. Mufti Islah, 'Pellets Injured 16 Jammu and Kashmir Personnel Too: Amnesty Report', News 18, 14 September 2017, https://www.news18.com/news/india/pellets-injured-16-jammu-and-kashmir-police-personnel-too-amnesty-report-1518019.html
85. Mudasir Ahmad, 'Losing Sight in Kashmir: Amnesty Report Highlights Trauma of Pellet-Gun Victims', The Wire, 14 September 2017, https://thewire.in/government/losing-sight-in-kashmir-amnesty-report-highlights-trauma-of-pellet-gun-victims
86. 'Today in History – April 22', Library of Congress, https://www.loc.gov/item/today-in-history/april-22/
87. Pallavi Gogoi, 'As a Young Journalist in India, I Was raped by M.J. Akbar. Here Is My Story', *The Washington Post*, 1 November 2018, https://www.washingtonpost.com/news/global-opinions/wp/2018/11/01/as-a-young-journalist-in-india-i-was-raped-by-m-j-akbar-here-is-my-story/
88. 'Full Text: Priya Ramani Acquitted in MJ Akbar Defamation Case; FP Report Cited in Verdict', Firstpost, 17 February 2021, https://www.firstpost.com/india/priya-ramani-acquitted-in-mj-akbar-defamation-case-judge-cites-fp-report-in-91-page/1
89. Audrey Carlsen et al., '#MeToo Brought Down 201 Powerful Men. Nearly Half of Their Replacements Are Women', *The New York Times*, 29 October 2018, https://www.nytimes.com/interactive/2018/10/23/us/metoo-replacements.html
90. 'Report on NHRC Mission to Assam's Detention Centres from 22 to 24 January, 2018', Cjp.org, 26 March 2018, https://cjp.org.in/wp-content/uploads/2018/11/NHRC-Report-Assam-Detention-Centres-26-3-2018-1.pdf
91. Rahul Karmakar, 'Over 19 Lakh Excluded from Assam's final NRC', *The Hindu*, 4 December 2021, https://www.thehindu.com/news/national/over-19-lakh-excluded-from-assams-final-nrc/article29307099.ece

92. 'Two years of Assam NRC: Uncertainty Looms over Re-verification Process', *Economic Times*, 31 August 2021, https://economictimes.indiatimes.com/news/politics-and-nation/two-years-of-assam-nrc-uncertainty-looms-over-re-verification-process/articleshow/85797921.cms?from=mdr
93. Prabin Kalita, 'Assam Told to Free Non-Muslims from Detention Camps: MoS in Lok Sabha', *Times of India*, 5 February 2020, https://timesofindia.indiatimes.com/city/guwahati/assam-told-to-free-non-muslims-from-detention-camps-mos-in-lok-sabha/articleshow/73958268.cms
94. Rana Ayyub, 'The 100 Most Influential People of 2020', *Time*, 22 September 2020, https://time.com/collection/100-most-influential-people-2020/5888255/bilkis/
95. Katie O'Malley, 'How Black Lives Matter Protests Have Changed the World, a Month After George Floyd's Death', *Elle*, 25 June 2020, https://www.elle.com/uk/life-and-culture/culture/a32822672/black-lives-matter-protests-achievements-statues-police-reform/
96. Sabrina Tavernise and John Eligon, 'Voters Say Black Lives Matter Protests Were Important. They Disagree on Why', *The New York Times*, 7 November 2020, https://www.nytimes.com/2020/11/07/us/black-lives-matter-protests.html
97. 'Protests Continue in Gujarat Over Thrashing of Dalits Near Una', *The Hindu*, 21 July 2016, https://www.thehindu.com/news/national/Una-incident-Protests-continue-in-Gujarat/article60574263.ece?homepage=true
98. Chetan Chauhan, 'Centre Bans Sale of Cows for Slaughter at Animal Markets, Restricts Cattle Trade', *Hindustan Times*, 19 July 2017, https://www.hindustantimes.com/india-news/centre-bans-cow-slaughter-across-india-cows-can-be-sold-only-to-farmers/story-8sFXJxiNmZ8eD6NXDgbvnL.html
99. 'Violent Cow Protection in India', Human Rights Watch, 18 February 2019, https://www.hrw.org/report/2019/02/18/violent-cow-protection-india/vigilante-groups-attack-minorities

100. Shoaib Daniyal, '"Your Mother, You Take Care of it": Meet the Dalits behind Gujarat's stirring cow carcass protests', Scroll. in, 23 July 2016, https://scroll.in/article/812329/your-mother-you-take-care-of-it-meet-the-dalits-behind-gujarats-stirring-cow-carcass-protests
101. The Wire, 'Dalit Family Stripped, Beaten As "Gau Raksha" Vigilantism Continues', 13 July 2016, https://thewire.in/politics/dalit-family-stripped-beaten-as-gau-raksha-vigilantism-continues
102. Aarefa Johari, 'An Assault on Dalits May Have Triggered the Biggest Lower-Caste Uprising in Gujarat in 30 Years', Scroll.in, 20 July 2016, https://scroll.in/article/812100/an-assault-on-dalits-may-have-triggered-the-biggest-lower-caste-uprising-in-gujarat-in-30-years
103. Shuchi Kapoor, 'When Dalits Threw Away Cow Carcasses and Upended Hierarchies in Gujarat', *Economic Times,* 21 August 2016, https://m.economictimes.com/news/politics-and-nation/when-dalits-threw-away-cow-carcasses-and-upended-hierarchies-in-gujarat/amp_articleshow/53788531.cms
104. 'Attack Me If You Want, Not My Dalit Brothers: PM Narendra Modi Slams "fake" Gau Rakshaks Again', Firstpost, 8 August 2016, https://www.firstpost.com/politics/attack-me-if-you-want-not-my-dalit-brothers-pm-narendra-modi-slams-fake-gau-rakshaks-again-2941540.html
105. 'Dholka Authorities Begin Land Measurement at Saroda village', *The Indian Express,* 21 September 2016, https://indianexpress.com/article/india/india-news-india/dholka-authorities-begin-land-measurement-at-saroda-village-3041564/
106. 'Una Effect: Gujarat to Set Up 16 Special Courts to Handle SC/ST Atrocity Cases', *Hindustan Times,* 22 September 2016, https://www.hindustantimes.com/india-news/una-effect-gujarat-to-set-up-16-special-courts-to-handle-sc-st-atrocity-cases/story-FMqKQp5pFmEkVBIVF0rxOO.html

107. Damayantee Dhar, 'First Conviction by Gujarat's Special SC/ST Atrocity Courts Offers Ray of Hope to Many Victims', The Wire, 8 May 2017, https://thewire.in/caste/gujarat-caste-special-courts
108. Arghya Bhaskar, 'Jharkhand and Homes Without Maps: Puny Process of Clearance at the Heart of This Mammoth Developmental Issue', Firstpost, 2 February 2021, https://www.firstpost.com/india/jharkhand-and-homes-without-maps-puny-process-of-clearance-at-the-heart-of-this-mammoth-developmental-issue-9263971.html
109. Aakar Patel, 'The Weak Case That Kept Stan Swamy in Jail, Where He Died', Deccan Chronicle, 13 July 2021, https://www.deccanchronicle.com/opinion/columnists/120721/the-weak-case-that-kept-stan-swamy-in-jail-where-he-died.html
110. Jitendra, 'Amendments to Century-Old Laws on Tribal Rights Spark Protests in Jharkhand', DownToEarth, 24 November 2016, https://www.downtoearth.org.in/news/governance/amendments-to-century-old-tribal-rights-laws-spark-protests-in-jharkhand-56411
111. 'Make in India: Jharkhand Government Claims to Have Attracted Investment Worth Rs 62,000 cr', The Indian Express, 17 February 2016, https://indianexpress.com/article/india/india-news-india/jharkhand-govt-claims-to-have-attracted-investment-worth-rs-62000-cr/
112. Abhishek Angad, 'Explained: What Is the Pathalgadi Movement, and What Is JMM Govt's Stand on It', The Indian Express, 23 December 2020, https://indianexpress.com/article/explained/explained-what-is-pathalgadi-movement-and-what-is-the-jmm-govts-stand-on-this-7114979/
113. Supriya Sharma, '10,000 People Charged with Sedition in One Jharkhand District. What Does Democracy Mean Here', Scroll.in, 19 November 2019, https://scroll.in/article/944116/10000-

people-charged-with-sedition-in-one-jharkhand-district-what-does-democracy-mean-here

114. 'Jharkhand: Rights Body Urges Govt to Withdraw Cases Against Thousands of Tribals', The Wire, 11 October 2019, https://thewire.in/rights/jharkhand-rights-body-urges-govt-to-withdraw-cases-against-thousands-of-tribals

115. Asmita Gaire, 'Free Report: Friday for Future in Sai Global College', Tunza Eco Generation, 28 December 2019, https://tunza.eco-generation.org/ambassadorReportView.jsp?viewID=48571

116. Dana R. Fisher, 'The Broader Importance of #FridaysForFuture', Nature Climate Change, Volume 9, Number 430-431 (2019), https://www.nature.com/articles/s41558-019-0484-y

117. 'Climate Activist Greta Thunberg Turns 18', Thomson Reuters, 30 September 2021, https://reuters.screenocean.com/record/1639485

118. Taran Deol, 'All About the 3 Modi Govt Ordinances Haryana Farmers Are Protesting Against', The Print, 12 September 2020, https://theprint.in/theprint-essential/all-about-the-3-modi-govt-ordinances-haryana-farmers-are-protesting-against/501227/

119. 'Farming and Farm Income', Economic Research Service, 3 June 2022, https://www.ers.usda.gov/data-products/ag-and-food-statistics-charting-the-essentials/farming-and-farm-income/

120. 'India at a Glance', Food and Agriculture Organization of the United Nations, https://www.fao.org/india/fao-in-india/india-at-a-glance/en/

121. Vishnu Padhmanabhan, 'The Land Challenge Underlying India's Farm Crisis', Mint, 15 October 2018, https://www.livemint.com/Politics/SOG43o5ypqO13j0QflaawM/The-land-challenge-underlying-Indias-farm-crisis.html

122. Shoaib Daniyal, 'Dubious Voice Vote to Pass Critical Farm Bills Severely Dents Indian Democracy', Scroll.in, 20 September 2020,

https://scroll.in/article/973588/use-of-a-dubious-voice-vote-to-pass-critical-farm-bills-severely-dents-indian-democracy.

123. 'Situation Assessment Survey of Agricultural Households: NSS 70th Round, Schedule 33, January-December 2013 (Visit 1)', National Sample Survey Office, 23 May 2015, http://www.icssrdataservice.in/datarepository/index.php/catalog/104

124. Harish Pullanoor, ed., 'Farmers Don't Know What They Want, What Is Wrong with Laws: Hema Malini', NDTV, 13 January 2021, https://www.ndtv.com/india-news/farmers-dont-know-what-they-want-someone-else-behind-protest-hema-malini-2351719

125. C K Manoj, 'Bihar Scrapped APMC Act, Mandi System 14 Years Ago; Here's What It Did to Farmers', DownToEarth, 7 December 2020, https://www.downtoearth.org.in/news/agriculture/bihar-scrapped-apmc-act-mandi-system-14-years-ago-here-s-what-it-did-to-farmers-74534

126. Shekhar Gupta, 'Modi's Dilemma: Will Farmer Protests Be His Thatcher or Anna Hazare Moment?', Business Standard, 5 December 2020, https://www.business-standard.com/article/opinion/modi-s-dilemma-anna-or-thatcher-120120401543_1.html

127. Zia Haq, 'Modi Govt Readies to Cut Flab Out of UPA's Flagship Food Security Law', *Hindustan Times*, 2 February 2015, https://www.hindustantimes.com/india/modi-govt-readies-to-cut-flab-out-of-upa-s-flagship-food-security-law/story-yUhRKpO6yTz2Ms1ChOPLfO.html

128. Sachin Kumar Jain, 'For India, the Fight at WTO Will Be About Food Security', DownToEarth, 9 December 2017, https://www.downtoearth.org.in/news/economy/why-india-needs-to-fight-for-food-security-at-wto-59310

129. 'Canada Has 18 Sikh MPs, India Only 13 in Lok Sabha', *Times Of India*, 23 October 2019, https://timesofindia.indiatimes.com/india/canada-has-18-sikh-mps-india-only-13-in-lok-sabha/articleshow/71714142.cms

130. Kallol Bhattacherjee, 'India Summons Canadian High Commissioner; Issues Demarche Over Trudeau's Remarks', *The Hindu*, 4 December 2020, https://www.thehindu.com/news/national/farmers-protest-india-summons-canadian-high-commissioner-issues-demarche-over-trudeaus-remarks/article33248578.ece
131. 'Agitating Farmers Hand Over Letter to Centre, Demand Special Parliament Session to Repeal New Farm Laws', Zee News, 3 December 2020, https://zeenews.india.com/india/agitating-farmers-hand-over-letter-to-centre-demand-special-parliament-session-to-repeal-new-farm-laws-2328305.html
132. '"Theatre of the Absurd": Political Parties Across Spectrum Condemn Disha Ravi's Arrest', *The Week*, 15 February 2021, https://www.theweek.in/news/india/2021/02/15/theatre-of-the-absurd-political-parties-across-spectrum-condemn-disha-ravi-arrest.html
133. Satya Prakash, '"Extremely Disappointed", Supreme Court Raps Govt Over Impasse', 12 January 2021, https://www.tribuneindia.com/news/nation/extremely-disappointed-supreme-court-raps-govt-over-impasse-197085
134. 'The Power of 3: How 3 SC Judges Took Centre to School Over 3 Farm Laws', *India Today*, 12 January 2021, https://www.indiatoday.in/india/story/farm-laws-stay-supreme-court-verdict-quotes-infographic-1758353-2021-01-12
135. '"We Are Extremely Disappointed at the Way Govt. Handling the Farmers Protests and Farm Laws", Chief Justice Bobde', LiveLaw.in, 11 January 2021, https://www.livelaw.in/amp/top-stories/farmers-protests-and-farm-laws-supreme-court-cji-bobde-168233
136. Deepali Sharma, ed., 'Supreme Court-Appointed Committee on Farm Laws Submits Its Report, Hearing on the Matter Scheduled for April 5', *Hindustan Times*, 31 March 2021, https://www.hindustantimes.com/india-news/supreme-court-appointed-three-

member-committee-on-the-three-new-farm-laws-submits-its-report-to-the-sc-in-a-sealed-cover-101617178915628.html.
137. 'Lok Sabha Unstarred Question No. 3418 to Be Answered on 13th March 2020', Government of India, http://164.100.24.220/loksabhaquestions/annex/173/AU3418.pdf
138. Tabassum Barnagarwala, 'Maharashtra: Govt Hikes ASHA Supervisors' Salary by Rs 1,000; Foot Soldiers Unhappy', *The Indian Express*, 26 June 2020, https://indianexpress.com/article/india/maharashtra-govt-hikes-asha-supervisors-salary-by-rs-1000-foot-soldiers-unhappy-6476637/
139. Kamaldeep Singh Brar, 'Paid a Pittance, ASHAs Forced to Buy or Borrow Smartphones for Covid Survey', *The Indian Express*, 25 June 2020, https://indianexpress.com/article/cities/chandigarh/paid-a-pittance-ashas-forced-to-buy-or-borrow-smartphones-for-covid-survey-6475493/
140. Ilangovan Rajasekaran, 'Alarming Act', *Frontline*, 3 October 2014, https://frontline.thehindu.com/the-nation/alarming-act/article6412617.ece
141. 'Manish Tiwari: Because POTA Was Misused, Advani Initiated Its Repeal', *BusinessLine*, 23 July 2019, https://www.thehindubusinessline.com/news/national/manish-tiwari-because-pota-was-misused-advani-initiated-its-repeal/article28691056.ece
142. 'Anti-Terrorism Legislation', Human Rights Watch, 20 November 2001, https://www.hrw.org/legacy/backgrounder/asia/india-bck1121.htm
143. PTI, 'Modi Slams Centre for Rejecting Anti-terror Bill GUJCOC', *The Economic Times*, 17 August 2009, https://economictimes.indiatimes.com/news/politics-and-nation/modi-slams-centre-for-rejecting-anti-terror-bill-gujcoc/articleshow/4901929.cms?from=mdr
144. TNN, 'Activists Want President to Strike Down GujCTOC Bill', *Times of India*, 6 October 2015, https://timesofindia.indiatimes.

com/city/vadodara/activists-want-president-to-strike-down-gujctoc-bill/articleshow/49241261.cms?from=mdr
145. Saikat Datta, '1,528 Fake Encounters in Manipur Alone: Why the Supreme Court Judgement on AFSPA Matters', Scroll.in, 11 July 2016, https://scroll.in/article/811521/supreme-court-judgement-on-afspa-sets-stage-for-huge-improvement-in-indias-human-rights-situation
146. Chander Suta Dogra, 'Truth, Exhumed', *Outlook*, 5 February 2022, https://www.outlookindia.com/magazine/story/truth-exhumed/278182
147. www.rti-rating.org
148. Neha Alawadhi, 'India Had Highest Number of Internet Shutdowns at 109 in 2020: Report', *Business Standard*, 4 March 2021, https://www.business-standard.com/article/current-affairs/india-had-highest-number-of-internet-shutdowns-at-109-in-2020-report-121030301203_1.html
149. Prabhash K Dutta, 'Internet Access a Fundamental Right, Supreme Court Makes It Official: Article 19 Explained', *India Today*, 10 January 2020, https://www.indiatoday.in/news-analysis/story/internet-access-fundamental-right-supreme-court-makes-official-article-19-explained-1635662-2020-01-10
150. Lata Jha, '17 OTT Platforms Release Self-Regulation Toolkit', *Mint*, 12 February 2021, https://www.livemint.com/industry/media/ott-services-release-tool-kit-for-selfregulation-11613035662795.html
151. '"Love Jihad" Not Defined under Law, Says Centre', *The Hindu*, 17 November 2020, https://www.thehindu.com/news/national/love-jihad-not-defined-under-law-says-centre/article30736760.ece
152. Ashwani Sharma, 'Himachal's New Anti-conversion Law Has An Old Provision Quashed By High Court', *The Indian Express*, 19 September 2019, https://indianexpress.com/article/india/

himachal-pradesh-new-anti-conversion-law-has-an-old-provision-quashed-by-high-court-6009421/

153. Mahesh Langa, 'Gujarat Assembly Passes 'Love Jihad' Law', *The Hindu*, 2 April 2021, https://www.thehindu.com/news/national/other-states/gujarat-assembly-passes-love-jihad-law/article34217780.ece

154. Chaitanya Mallapur, 'Why New Bill Meant to Benefit Transgender People Is Termed Regressive', IndiaSpend, 22 August 2019, https://www.indiaspend.com/why-new-bill-meant-to-benefit-transgender-people-is-termed-regressive/

155. 'Lok Sabha Passes Bill to Exempt Political Parties from Scrutiny on Foreign Funds, Without Debate', *The Hindu*, 18 March 2018, https://www.thehindu.com/news/national/lok-sabha-passes-bill-to-exempt-political-parties-from-scrutiny-on-foreign-funds-without-debate/article23285764.ece

156. M.K. Venu, 'Revealed: Jaitley Redefines "Foreign" as "Indian" to Get BJP, Congress Off the Hook for FCRA Violation', The Wire, 2 April 2016, https://m.thewire.in/article/government/revealed-jaitley-gifts-bjp-congress-a-clean-chit-retrospectively-on-fcra-violation/amp

157. 'India's Crackdown on NGOs, in Four Charts', *Mint*, 30 September 2020, https://www.livemint.com/news/india/india-s-crackdown-on-ngos-in-four-charts-11601363086584.html

158. 'Crackdown Has NGOs' Foreign Funding Reduce 40 pc in Four Years: Report', *Deccan Chronicle*, 11 March 2019, https://www.deccanchronicle.com/business/in-other-news/110319/crackdown-has-ngos-foreign-funding-reduce-40-pc-in-four-years-report.html

159. 'Land Acq. Under CBA Act 1957', Ministry of Coal, 22 July 2021, https://coal.gov.in/major-statistics/land-acq-under-cba-act-1957

160. Ishan Kukreti, 'Tribal Ministry Tells States to Stop Rejecting FRA Claims on Invalid Grounds', DownToEarth, 23 July 2018, https://

www.downtoearth.org.in/news/forests/tribal-ministry-tells-states-to-stop-rejecting-fra-claims-on-invalid-grounds-61214

161. Aakar Patel, 'Excuse Me, May I Have Your House', *Outlook*, 4 February 2022, https://www.outlookindia.com/website/story/excuse-me-may-i-have-your-house/296626

162. Sima Kotecha, 'India Covid: How Law Stops NGOs Distributing Essential Aid', BBC News, 13 May 2021, https://www.bbc.com/news/world-asia-india-57095591

163. Jitendra, 'New Poverty Line: Rs 32 for Rural India, Rs 47 for Urban India', DownToEarth, 8 July 2014, https://www.downtoearth.org.in/news/new-poverty-line-rs-32-for-rural-india-rs-47-for-urban-india-45134

164. Ritika Chopra, 'Calorie Intake of the Rural Poor Has Drastically Fallen, Says Planning Commission Report', *India Today*, 22 October 2011, https://www.indiatoday.in/india/north/story/poverty-malnutrition-india-hunger-index-143926-2011-10-22

165. 'Consumer Spending Declines for First Time in Four Decades', *The Economic Times*, 16 November 2019, https://economictimes.indiatimes.com/news/economy/indicators/consumer-spending-declines-for-first-time-in-four-decades/articleshow/72069291.cms

166. 'Global Hunger Index Scores By 2021 GHI Rank', Global Hunger Index, https://www.globalhungerindex.org/ranking.html

167. 'National Family Health Survey, India', http://rchiips.org/nfhs/

168. 'All You Wanted to Know About MNREGA', *BusinessLine*, 12 January 2018, https://www.thehindubusinessline.com/opinion/columns/slate/all-you-wanted-to-know-about-mgnrega/article9539721.ece

169. '230 Million Indians Pushed into Poverty amid Covid-19 Pandemic: Report', *Business Standard*, 6 May 2021, https://www.business-standard.com/article/economy-policy/230-million-indians-pushed-into-poverty-amid-covid-19-pandemic-report-121050600751_1.html

170. Nivedita Rao, 'Malnutrition in India: The National Nutrition Startegy Explained', PRS Legislative Research, 8 September 2017, https://prsindia.org/theprsblog/malnutrition-in-india-the-national-nutrition-strategy-explained?page=232&per-page=1
171. 'Fact Sheet: Child Labour in India', International Labour Organization, 8 June 2017, https://www.ilo.org/newdelhi/whatwedo/publications/WCMS_557089/lang--en/index.htm
172. '"Lost Generation" Fears As COVID Locks Out India's Poor Students', Aljazeera, 5 August 2021, https://www.aljazeera.com/news/2021/8/5/children-covid-india-poor-students-digital-divide
173. Sagnik Chowdhury, '30% Women Married Under Age 18', *The Indian Express*, 31 May 2016, https://indianexpress.com/article/explained/child-marriage-women-india-census-data-2011-2826398/
174. 'Social, Economic and Educational Status of the Muslim Community of India', Government of India, November 2006, https://minorityaffairs.gov.in/sites/default/files/sachar_comm.pdf
175. 'Need to Include Dalit Christians and Muslims in the List of Scheduled Castes', IndiaKanoon, 29 August 2011, https://indiankanoon.org/doc/60551365/
176. 'India Justice Report 2019', Tata Trusts, October 2019, https://www.tatatrusts.org/upload/pdf/overall-report-single.pdf
177. 'Who Tells Our Stories Matters', Oxfam India, 2 August 2019, https://www.oxfamindia.org/sites/default/files/201908/Oxfam%20NewsLaundry%20Report_For%20Media%20use.pdf

ABOUT THE AUTHOR

Aakar Patel is a writer and human rights activist based in Bangalore. He is chair of Amnesty International India.

ABOUT THE ILLUSTRATOR

PenPencilDraw is an anonymous political satirist.